CGP — books like no others!

CGP

# Gear up for 9-1 GCSE English with CGP!

If you want to do well in your GCSE English Language and English Literature exams, good writing is pretty important. To put it mildly.

Now, here at CGP, we know what examiners like. And in this fantastic book, we spill the beans on all the skills you'll need to pick up top marks!

It's packed with advice, explanations and examples — plus practice questions to put you through your paces. All in all, it's well worth writing home about.

# CGP — still the best! ☺

Our sole aim here at CGP is to produce the highest quality books — carefully written, immaculately presented and dangerously close to being funny.

Then we work our socks off to get them out to you — at the cheapest possible prices.

# CONTENTS

## Section One — The Basics

## Section Two — Writing About Texts

# CONTENTS

## Section Three — Writing Non-Fiction

## Section Four — Creative Writing

Published by CGP

Editors:
Joe Brazier
Emma Crighton

With thanks to Holly Robinson for the proofreading and Jan Greenway for the copyright research.

ISBN: 978 1 84762 890 9

Printed by Elanders Ltd, Newcastle upon Tyne.
Clipart from Corel®

Based on the classic CGP style created by Richard Parsons.

# Writing for GCSE English

You'll have to do lots of types of writing for GCSE English Language and GCSE English Literature. Luckily, we've got some first-rate tips to help you reach all-round writing perfection.

## This book is all about writing

1) This book is full of <u>handy tips</u> for writing about novels, plays, poetry and non-fiction.

2) It also has advice about <u>writing your own</u> non-fiction and creative writing.

3) This <u>first section</u> will focus on the <u>basics</u> of <u>writing</u>. Then the <u>rest</u> of the book will give you advice about answering specific <u>types</u> of questions.

*Iris had been practising different types of writing for her exam.*

## There are different types of writing for English Language

1) For <u>English Language</u>, you'll be given short extracts from fiction and non-fiction texts that you've never seen before. You'll have to write some <u>answers</u> to questions about the extracts. Here's an <u>example question</u>:

> Read the article about Lake Nakuru National Park. How does the writer use language to advise tourists about visiting the park?

*See page 2 and Section 2 (p.26-30) for more about answering these questions.*

2) You will also have to write your <u>own texts</u>. For example, you might have to write a story, description, letter, leaflet, article or review. Here's an <u>example question</u>:

> 'Writing with a pen or pencil is old-fashioned and time-consuming. Students should take all their exams using computers.'
> Write an article for a broadsheet newspaper in which you explain your point of view on this statement.

*There's more about writing your own texts in Section 3 and Section 4.*

## You'll write about fiction texts for English Literature

1) If you're taking <u>English Literature</u>, you'll write about <u>different types</u> of texts, e.g. poetry, novels and plays.

2) You'll have to write <u>essays</u> about some <u>texts</u> that you've <u>studied</u> in your English lessons:

- A <u>Shakespeare play</u>
- A <u>19th-century novel</u>
- A modern <u>play</u> or <u>novel</u> (written after 1914)
- An anthology of <u>poetry</u> written between 1789 and now

3) You'll also have to write about some <u>unseen texts</u>, which might include:

- <u>Two unseen poems</u> that you have to compare.
- <u>One unseen poem</u>, which you have to <u>compare</u> with a poem you <u>have</u> studied.
- An <u>extract</u> from a <u>novel</u> or <u>play</u>, which you'll <u>compare</u> with a text you've studied.

*See page 3 and Section 2 (p.31-39) for more on writing English Literature essays.*

# English Language Reading Questions

For the reading questions in your English Language exams, you'll have to write some long answers about the text extracts you're given. Conveniently, there's some handy advice on this page for doing just that.

## You'll be given different types of text

1) You'll have to write about both <u>fiction</u> and <u>non-fiction</u> texts for English Language.

2) You'll be asked questions about things like the writer's <u>point of view</u>, how <u>effective</u> the texts are and the effects of the <u>language</u> and <u>structure</u> they use.

3) You might also have to <u>summarise</u> or <u>compare</u> two texts.

*There's more about comparing texts on pages 24-25.*

4) To <u>answer</u> these questions, you'll need to write <u>well-structured</u> long answers, using <u>full sentences</u> and <u>paragraphs</u>.

## Long answers need to have a clear structure

1) For the questions worth <u>fewer marks</u>, there's no need to write an <u>introduction</u> or a <u>conclusion</u> — you should just focus on writing <u>good points</u> that clearly <u>answer</u> the <u>question</u>.

2) You could use the <u>P.E.E.D.</u> structure to write your points (see pages 4-5) and make <u>one good point</u> per <u>paragraph</u>.

3) For the questions worth <u>lots of marks</u> (especially those that ask you to <u>evaluate</u> or <u>compare</u> texts), it may be a good idea to write a <u>short</u> introduction and conclusion. For example, here's a short conclusion:

> Overall, I think the text is extremely effective at persuading the reader to donate money to the charity. The author's consistent use of rhetorical techniques builds up to engage the reader's emotions, showing that the only moral choice is to support the charity.

*Keep your introductions and conclusions short and to the point.*

## You don't need to plan for every answer

1) You <u>won't</u> need to <u>plan</u> every answer for the reading questions in English Language.

2) For the questions worth lots of marks though, it might help to <u>underline</u> any <u>key words</u> and jot down some <u>points</u> before you start writing. Just make sure you don't spend <u>too long</u> doing it.

> <u>How</u> does the writer use <u>language</u> to <u>persuade their audience</u> to agree with their opinions on <u>road safety</u>?

*You should always do a more detailed plan for the writing questions — see pages 48 and 50.*

> IDEAS:
> • Emotive language e.g. "absolute disgrace"
> • Technical language, facts and stats ("50% of road users...")
> • Imagery to scare reader — "broken bones" etc.

## *Make sure the conclusion isn't too long — bring a tape measure...*

English Language questions can be tricky, so it's a good idea to practise writing some exam-style answers in advance. Think about how you're structuring your answer, and make everything really clear to the examiner.

**Section One — The Basics**

# English Literature Essays

Here's some advice on what you'll be faced with, and how to handle it, for English Literature...

## You'll need to write essays for English Literature

1) For your English Literature exams, you'll be writing about <u>novels</u>, <u>plays</u> and <u>poems</u>.

2) The <u>questions</u> you'll have to answer will often be about a particular <u>theme</u>, <u>character</u>, <u>mood</u> or <u>setting</u>. You'll need to write about the <u>techniques</u> the writer uses in your answers.

3) Some questions will also ask you to <u>compare</u> two texts — see pages 24-25.

4) For most English Literature questions, you'll need to write <u>essay</u> answers.

## The four basic steps for writing an essay

You can tackle any essay if you follow these <u>four steps</u>:

1) Work out what the question <u>MEANS</u>. <u>Read</u> the question carefully, and try to <u>understand</u> what it's asking you to do (see p.10-11).

2) Make your <u>PLAN</u>. Think about the <u>points</u> you want to make in your answer, and note down the <u>examples</u> you're going to use to back them up. See p.12-13 for more.

3) Use your plan to think of a <u>MAIN IDEA</u> — the most important <u>point</u> you're trying to make in your essay. Have a look at p.14-15 for more about this.

4) <u>WRITE</u> your answer. Don't forget to include an <u>introduction</u> (see p.18-19) and a <u>conclusion</u> (see p.22-23).

## There are three main parts to an essay

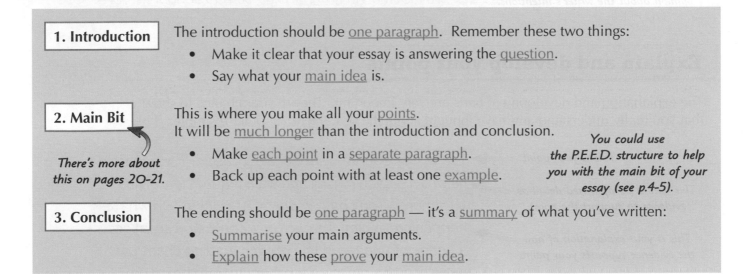

**1. Introduction**

The introduction should be <u>one paragraph</u>. Remember these two things:
- Make it clear that your essay is answering the <u>question</u>.
- Say what your <u>main idea</u> is.

**2. Main Bit**

*There's more about this on pages 20-21.*

This is where you make all your <u>points</u>.
It will be <u>much longer</u> than the introduction and conclusion.
- Make <u>each point</u> in a <u>separate paragraph</u>.
- Back up each point with at least one <u>example</u>.

*You could use the P.E.E.D. structure to help you with the main bit of your essay (see p.4-5).*

**3. Conclusion**

The ending should be <u>one paragraph</u> — it's a <u>summary</u> of what you've written:
- <u>Summarise</u> your main arguments.
- <u>Explain</u> how these <u>prove</u> your <u>main idea</u>.

## Practice Questions

1) "You should spend a long time planning your English Language answers." — true or false?

2) What are the four basic steps for writing essays?

3) What two things should you do in the conclusion of your essay?

# P.E.E.D.

P.E.E.D. is one of the most important techniques to use whenever you're writing about a text. You should use it to make well-structured points that clearly answer the question.

## P.E.E.D. is how to put your argument together

1) <u>P.E.E.D.</u> stands for:

**P**oint — Make a <u>point</u> to answer the question you've been given.

*Remember to start a new paragraph every time you make a new point.*

**E**xample — Then give an <u>example</u> from the text — either a <u>quote</u> or a <u>paraphrased detail</u> (a description of something from the text in your own words).

*Rover used P.E.E.D. to prove which lamp posts belonged to him.*

**E**xplain — After that, <u>explain how</u> your example <u>backs up</u> your point.

**D**evelop — Finally, <u>develop</u> your point — this might involve saying what the <u>effect on the reader</u> is, saying what the <u>writer's intention</u> is, <u>linking</u> your point to another part of the text or giving your <u>own opinion</u>.

2) Here's an example answer that includes those <u>four</u> things:

*This is your point.* ⟹
*This is your example, a quote from the text.* ⟹
*This bit is your explanation.* ⟹
*Here's your development — it gives an opinion about the writer's intentions.* ⟹

> The writer feels quite angry about school dinners. She says school food is "unappetising, unidentifiable and unacceptable". The repetition of 'un' emphasises her negative opinion about the quality of the food. I think the writer's intention is to show that children are justified in not wanting to eat school dinners.

## Explain and develop your points

The <u>explanation</u> and <u>development</u> parts are very important. They're your chance to show that you <u>really understand</u> and have <u>thought about</u> the text. Here's another <u>example</u>:

*This is your point.* ⟶
*This uses a paraphrased detail as evidence to support the point.* ⟶
*This is your explanation of how the evidence supports your point.* ⟶
*This develops the point by writing about the effect on the reader.* ⟶

> The writer sounds as if he is confused. For example, he starts each paragraph with a question, giving the impression that he doesn't understand what's happening to him. The writer's confusion creates a sense of unease in the reader, leading them to question their own understanding of the issue.

## Oi — stop giggling at the back...

P.E.E.D. is also called P.Q.D. (Point, Quote, Discuss), P.Q.C. (Point, Quote, Comment), P.E.E.R. (Point, Example, Explain, Relate), or S.E.C. (Statement, Example, Comment). I chose P.E.E.D. because it tickles me...

# P.E.E.D.

P.E.E.D. will help you to pick up marks when you're writing about texts for both English Language and English Literature. It might even help you pick up marks in other subjects, but don't tell them I told you...

## P.E.E.D. is perfect for your literature essays

P.E.E.D. is really important for a good literature essay.

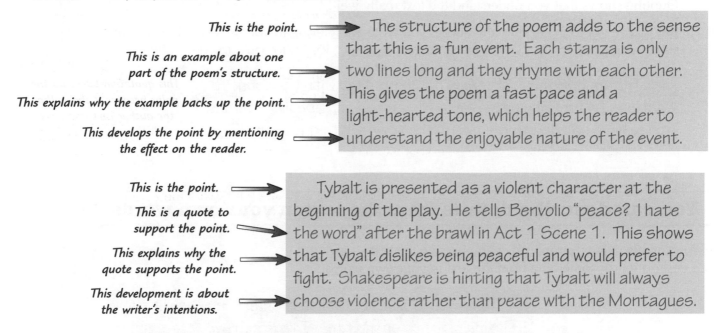

*This is the point.* → The structure of the poem adds to the sense that this is a fun event. Each stanza is only two lines long and they rhyme with each other. This gives the poem a fast pace and a light-hearted tone, which helps the reader to understand the enjoyable nature of the event.

*This is an example about one part of the poem's structure.* →

*This explains why the example backs up the point.* →

*This develops the point by mentioning the effect on the reader.* →

*This is the point.* → Tybalt is presented as a violent character at the beginning of the play. He tells Benvolio "peace? I hate the word" after the brawl in Act 1 Scene 1. This shows that Tybalt dislikes being peaceful and would prefer to fight. Shakespeare is hinting that Tybalt will always choose violence rather than peace with the Montagues.

*This is a quote to support the point.* →

*This explains why the quote supports the point.* →

*This development is about the writer's intentions.* →

## P.E.E.D. can be used for writing about non-fiction too

These are examples of P.E.E.D. in answers about non-fiction texts.

*This is the point.* → The leaflet uses language to appeal to young children. For example, it uses positive adjectives such as "fun" and "exciting". These make the activity sound friendly to children, so they are more likely to want to take part.

*This is an example about the language of the text.* →

*This explains why the example backs up the point.* →

*This develops the point by explaining how it persuades the reader to take part in the activity.* →

*This is the point.* → The writer uses second-person pronouns to advise the reader. The pronouns "you" and "your" are used throughout the text, which makes it seem as if the advice is directly aimed at the reader. This helps the writer to advise their audience, because the reader is more likely to consider the advice carefully if they think it is aimed directly at them.

*These are examples of the language in the text.* →

*This explains why the examples back up the point.* →

*This development explains how the text advises the reader.* →

## Practice Questions

1)  What does P.E.E.D. stand for and what does each word mean?

2)  Name two things that you can use as 'examples' when you're using P.E.E.D.

3)  Find a poem you like. Write three P.E.E.D. paragraphs giving different reasons why it's a good poem.

# Quoting and Evidence

Writing a good answer is a bit like a criminal trial... just with fewer wigs. You need evidence to convince the jury that someone is guilty, and you need evidence to convince the examiner that your points are valid.

## Give evidence for your points by quoting

1) Quoting shows that you understand the text really well.

2) But you've got to make sure any quotes you write are relevant to your answer. Don't quote something just because you know it. To get top marks, it's got to back up your point.

> The author of the article is not impressed with the council's actions so far. She says she is "disgusted and appalled" that they have not done more about the town's litter problem.

*This quotation backs up the point because it shows that the author isn't impressed with the council's actions.*

## You can describe details from the text in your own words

You can also give examples by paraphrasing the text — giving a description of something from the text in your own words.

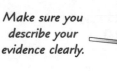
*Make sure you describe your evidence clearly.*

> The writer quickly establishes that the beach is a relaxing place to spend time. This is achieved through the use of multiple long sentences in the opening paragraph, which give the text a smooth, slow pace. This gives the reader a sense of the calm atmosphere of the beach, and sets the tone for the rest of the story.

## You can use background information as evidence too

1) For some texts, it might be helpful to know when a text was written and what life was like at the time.

> 'Pride and Prejudice' was published in 1813, at a time when it wasn't socially acceptable for upper-class women to work. If they didn't get married, they usually had to rely on family members to support them.

2) If it's relevant, you could give a little bit of historical background to a text.

> 'Macbeth' was written during the reign of King James, who ruled over both Scotland and England.

*Remember — only write about the historical background if it's useful to your answer (or if the question asks about it).*

---

## *Quotations and tomatoes — they both have sources...*

I'll give you a moment to wipe the tears of laughter from your eyes... ready? Right — evidence is the name of the game when it comes to exam success, so get good at picking out quotes or examples from the text.

# Quoting and Evidence

There are a few technical points you need to get your head around in order to quote properly. It's not tricky stuff, but it's important that you get it right. You can find it all on this page though, so that's a relief.

## You must use speech marks for all real quotes

You need speech marks with all quotations — from novels, articles, plays or poems.

Frankenstein continually talks about his creation as a "monster" or a "devil".

*These one-word quotations must have speech marks.*

Dickens uses the weather conditions to set the scene in Chapter 3. "It was a rimy morning, and very damp."

*This is the bit you're quoting. Just stick it in as part of your ordinary paragraph.*

## Some quotes are trickier than others

1) Speech marks aren't just used for quotations. They're also used when characters speak in novels. It starts to get really confusing when there's a character speaking in the bit you want to quote.

   You need double speech marks at the start of the quotation.

   "Jack spoke loudly. 'This head is for the beast. It's a gift.' "

   *Every time a character speaks, put what they say in single speech marks.*

   Then you've got to put double speech marks at the end of the whole thing.

2) If you're quoting more than one line of poetry, put a "/" to show where a new line starts.

   The poet compares a soldier's skull to an egg: "the blown / and broken bird's egg of a skull".

3) If you're quoting from a play, you must make it clear who's speaking.

   When Mercutio is dying, he wishes "a plague a' both your houses!" He doesn't just blame his enemies for his death; he blames the feud between the Montagues and the Capulets.

### Practice Questions

1) Explain the difference between quoting from the text and paraphrasing.
2) "You don't need quote marks for short quotes." — true or false?
3) How should you use speech marks if a character is speaking in the part of the text you want to quote?

# Writing Well

Ah... the writing well. Lower your bucket in, fill it up, and drink down those cool, refreshing words. These pages are all about how to write top notch answers to reading questions for both English GCSEs.

## You must write in formal language

When you're answering <u>reading questions</u>, you need to write in <u>formal language</u>. That <u>doesn't</u> mean it's got to be full of <u>long</u>, <u>complicated</u> words — just imagine you're writing to someone <u>important</u>.

*Keep your writing simple and formal, as if you're talking to a teacher.*

The poem is full of images of suffering. Blake seems to see suffering as the main feature of human life. At the same time, he makes it clear that he believes that London itself is the cause of a lot of this suffering.

*Use phrases like "at the same time" to make your writing more interesting. (See the next page for more on linking words.)*

*Write about the author and the poem in the present tense, unless it's about an actual historical event.*

When writing formally, <u>never</u> use <u>slang words</u> or <u>text speak</u>. These really <u>don't</u> <u>impress</u> the examiner. Always check your <u>spelling</u>, <u>punctuation</u> and <u>grammar</u>, too.

## Use clear explaining words and phrases

1) You've got to use <u>explaining words</u> and <u>phrases</u> to make your answer <u>easy to follow</u>.

This means that...    This is because...    Another key point is...

The problem with this is....    The important thing is...

2) Use these phrases to help you <u>explain</u> what your points <u>mean</u>.
   You could use them <u>after</u> you've given your <u>examples</u> or to <u>introduce</u> a <u>new point</u>.

## You can also use negative phrases

You can use <u>negative phrases</u> if you're trying to <u>criticise an opinion</u> or <u>disagree with another argument</u>.

This does not mean that...    This is not the same as...

*If you do criticise someone — flowers and a hug soften the blow.*

## *Explaining words — a phrase I'm going through...*

Explaining your points will win you good marks — it shows the examiner that you understand the question and that you're answering it properly. Oh, and don't use text speak — you won't rofl when you get no marks.

# Writing Well

We're not quite finished with words yet. The other trick you need to practise is using linking words. These are the lovely helpful words that link different points of your answer together.

## You need to link different points together

1) Don't just jump from one point to the next — you need to <u>show</u> the examiner that your answer is <u>organised</u>.

2) For example, you can <u>divide</u> your work up into <u>numbered points</u>.

There are three main points... Firstly... Secondly... Finally....

*Make sure you start a new paragraph for each numbered point.*

## Use linking words for top marks

1) Using a <u>variety</u> of linking words will make your writing sound <u>interesting</u> and <u>professional</u>.

2) Here are some <u>examples</u>.

Furthermore...    Nevertheless...    Although...    Instead...

3) Don't forget these <u>useful phrases</u>, too.

Another view is....    Even though...    At the same time...    Despite this...

*Linking words and phrases are really useful for comparison questions — see pages 24-25 for more about this.*

## You can also use opposite phrases

Sometimes when you're arguing, you need to give <u>both sides of the argument</u> (see p.21). That's when you should use phrases <u>like these</u>.

On the one hand...    On the other hand...    One way...    Another way...

## Use however and therefore in the middle of sentences

This means, therefore, that...    Another view, however, is that...

### Practice Questions

1) Rewrite this sentence using formal language:
"The leaflet isn't gr8 cos it doesn't use cool language."

2) List three linking words that you could use in an essay to link your points together.

# Reading the Question

It's really important to carefully read and understand the questions before you start writing in the exams. You also need to think about which question you're going to pick when you have a choice of more than one.

## Your answer must match the question

1) To get a good mark, you need to do exactly what the question tells you to do.

2) Start by working out what the question really means.

3) To help you with this, you could underline any key words you spot.

4) If you really don't understand a question, don't panic — read it through a couple of times, and break the question down to work out exactly what it's asking you (see next page).

## Sometimes there'll be a choice of questions

1) If you have a choice of questions, pick one that you think you'll be able to write loads of interesting stuff about.

2) Don't rush into the first question you read — have a look at all the options before you decide.

Sometimes it's hard to narrow down your choices.

## Narrow down your choices

1) To decide which question to answer, read through the questions quickly.

2) Put a pencil mark beside any question you think you can answer.

3) Then work out exactly what these questions are asking you to do.

4) Finally, pick the ones you're going to answer.

> Make sure you know how many questions you're meant to answer.
> On some papers, you'll have a choice of questions in each section.

## Make sure you answer questions on the texts you've studied

1) You'll have studied some texts in class for your English Literature exams — so for these exams, you only need to read the questions that are about the texts you know.

2) You might have a choice of questions to answer for the text you've studied — so pick the one you think you can write the best answer for.

THINK before you decide.

---

### *Always read the paper — except in the loo...*

Phew. Seems like a big fuss over a few questions — but it's worth it. Choosing the right question is super important — pick the right one and you'll make it really easy for yourself to pick up lots of lovely marks.

# Reading the Question

This page has some examples of exam questions and what they mean.

## Here are some typical exam questions

1) This type of question is <u>very common</u> in the <u>poetry section</u> of your <u>English Literature</u> exam.

*You'll need to look at two poems and find similarities and differences between them.*

Compare how the poets show conflict in *Mametz Wood* and one other poem of your choice. Remember to refer to:
- what the poets write about conflict
- how the poets present conflict.

*This is the main focus of the question, so the points you make and the examples you use need to be relevant to 'conflict'.*

*You have to cover these points in your essay, so make sure you don't forget them.*

*You must write about the named poem, but you can choose the other poem. Make sure you choose a poem that you can link to the poem named in the question.*

2) You might get a question like <u>this</u> in your <u>English Literature</u> exam:

*You need to look at Meena — only write about other characters if they show something important about her.*

How does Syal present Meena as a brave character in *Anita and Me*? Remember to refer to:
- her words and actions
- the techniques Syal uses to show her bravery.

*This is the main focus of the question. Think of moments in the text when Meena shows bravery. You could also think of times when she isn't brave.*

*This means you'll need to give specific examples of what she does in the book.*

*Look at things like narrative viewpoint, descriptive language, etc.*

3) In your <u>English Language exams</u>, you might get asked about the effect of <u>language</u> in a text.

*You need to look at the language the leaflet uses and what effect it has.*

How does the writer use language in the leaflet 'Saving the future' to persuade the reader? Remember to refer to:
- the words and phrases the writer chooses
- the techniques the writer uses.

*Look at specific words and phrases in the leaflet and say what effect they have.*

*Write about the effects of techniques such as alliteration, irony and metaphors.*

4) You'll also have to do some of your <u>own writing</u> for your <u>English Language</u> exams.

*The text that you write needs to be in the style of a letter.*

Write a letter to your local council giving advice on how they might encourage more people to recycle.

*You need to advise your audience — see pages 42-43.*

*You need to write about how the council could get more people recycling.*

## Practice Questions

1) If you have a choice of questions about the text you've studied, which one should you choose?

2) How many questions do you have to answer in **your** exam?

3) If you've got to choose one of the poems for a comparison question, how should you pick?

# How to Plan

You'll need to do more detailed plans for your English Literature essays and the writing questions in your English Language exams. Planning might seem boring, but it's the best way to write a good answer.

## Planning will save you time later

Here are some <u>important reasons</u> why you should make a <u>plan</u>:

> 1) Your answer will <u>stick to the point</u> better. If you don't plan, your writing will wander and you won't answer the question properly.
>
> 2) You won't suddenly run out of things to write. <u>Never</u> rush into your writing <u>without</u> stopping and thinking first.
>
> 3) Planning helps you <u>sort</u> your ideas out and put them in a <u>clear order</u>. It'll help you write a <u>clear</u> answer.

*"Now it's time for my evil, organised and structured plan... mwuahaha!"*

1) You must <u>take time</u> to plan essays and writing questions, even if you feel like you're in a <u>rush</u>.

2) Even if the question <u>looks</u> easy, it's <u>still</u> important to make a plan. You <u>don't</u> want to <u>miss</u> a key point out of your answer.

<u>Don't worry</u> about what <u>other people</u> do — particularly in exams. Just concentrate on making your <u>plan</u>.

## Write down what you think is important

1) Write some <u>notes</u> on the <u>points</u> you want to make in your answer and think of <u>examples</u> you can use to <u>support</u> your points. Make sure that anything you note down is <u>relevant</u> to the question.

2) To make sure your answer has a <u>logical</u> structure, put your notes into some sort of <u>order</u> — you could do this by <u>numbering</u> each point on your <u>plan</u>.

3) Here's a question and an <u>example plan</u> for an English Literature essay.

> Write about the relationship between Mickey and Edward in *Blood Brothers*.

*If you decide not to use an idea, cross it out.*

*Number your points in the order you're going to write about them.*

1 They become friendly immediately after they meet, even though they don't know they're related — hints at their brotherly bond.

~~They meet each other by coincidence as children — influence of fate?~~

3 Tragic ending — their relationship deteriorates, then they both die.

2 They grow apart as their lives become more different — influence of social class and financial situation.

4) When you've got some <u>notes</u> and a <u>structure</u>, just <u>double check</u> that your plan is still <u>answering</u> the <u>question</u>. If it isn't then you need to <u>fix</u> it so that it does.

## *Plan it — make your writing out of this world...*

You might be sick of hearing this now, but... plan your answer. If you just start writing without a plan, then your points will be jumbled up, your argument won't be convincing, and you'll forget really important stuff.

# How to Plan

Look at the question you're going to answer carefully. Pick out the things it's asking you to do and think about how you can do those things correctly. The closer you stick to the question, the better you'll do.

## Use the question to make your plan

Here's a question and an example plan for an English Language writing task.

> Write an article for a teenage magazine to persuade other teenagers to give more help to homeless people. You should:
> * write an article for teenagers
> * explain why young people should help homeless people
> * write to persuade.

*The question tells you your audience (teenagers), the style you have to write in (an article) and the purpose of your writing (persuading). For more about writing non-fiction, see Section 3.*

*Sometimes there will be points under the question to give you ideas on what you need to write about.*

> Helping the Homeless — teenage magazine.
>
> * article in teenage magazine — need to write in style of an article. Tone and language needs to be for teenagers.
>
> * persuade — need to use persuasive techniques — direct address to reader, questions, exaggeration etc. Convince the reader to help the homeless.
>
> * why should young people help? — should help the needy, it's a good experience, will improve the town they live in etc.

*Scribble notes on what the question is asking you to do. Make sure you've thought about the points under the question.*

*Try to think of lots of good reasons. Then put them in order of importance. Start your article with the most important reason.*

## Use your plan to remind you of your points

1) The big reason for planning is so that you know what you're going to write, and you don't forget anything.

2) You can also use your plan to guide the examiner through your answer. For English Literature essays, it'll really impress the examiner if you can set out the points you're going to make in your introduction, like this:

> George Orwell uses the character of Napoleon to show how power corrupts leaders. He does this firstly by showing how Napoleon starts acting in his own interests once the pigs take over, and secondly, by showing how Napoleon becomes more extreme in his actions once he's all-powerful.

*This shows the examiner that you're going to talk about this point first...*

*...and then this point second.*

*See p.18-19 for more on introductions.*

## Practice Questions

1) What are the main benefits of planning your answer?

2) What are the bullet points underneath some questions for?

3) Plan an answer to the question 'Why plan?'

# Planning — Picking out Your Main Idea

For English Literature essays, it's useful to pick out a main idea — it'll help you stay focused when you write.

## You need to work out what your main idea is

1) The <u>main idea</u> of an English Literature essay is the overall <u>argument</u> or <u>point</u> that you want to get across to the examiner — your essay should be <u>focused</u> on that point.

2) You should mention your main idea in your <u>introduction</u> and <u>conclusion</u>, and you need to make sure each paragraph <u>supports</u> your main idea.

3) Here are some examples:

> How does Stevenson explore ideas of good and evil in *The Strange Case of Dr Jekyll and Mr Hyde*?

*Here your main idea might be that Stevenson thinks all of mankind have both good and evil inside.*

> How does Priestley present the character of Sheila in *An Inspector Calls*?

*Here your main idea might be that Sheila is presented as a caring character.*

## You need examples to back up your main idea

1) No one will ever agree with you if you haven't got <u>examples</u> (e.g. <u>quotations</u>) to <u>back up</u> your main idea.

2) When you <u>choose</u> your main idea, <u>make sure</u> you can <u>back it up</u> by <u>referring to the text</u>. You need to be able to make <u>three</u> or <u>four</u> good points that <u>support</u> your main idea.

3) If you were answering the question above about Sheila, you <u>could</u> make points like these:

> Sheila shows her caring nature when she is upset by the Inspector's description of Eva's death. She says that she "can't help thinking about this girl — destroying herself so horribly". This suggests that she has been deeply affected by the Inspector's story.

> Although Sheila gets Eva sacked, she didn't think it would cause anyone harm — she says it "didn't seem to be anything very terrible at the time". This shows that, while she can be careless, she doesn't intentionally want to hurt people.

*These points both support the main idea that Sheila is a caring character.*

4) Your <u>examples</u> must be <u>related</u> to your <u>main idea</u>, so that your <u>whole essay</u> provides <u>evidence</u> for your <u>main idea</u>.

## There's never only one right answer

1) Often there are <u>loads</u> of different main ideas.

2) Don't worry about getting the "<u>right</u>" one. If you can <u>back up</u> whatever you say using <u>examples</u> and <u>quotations</u> from the writing, you'll be fine.

3) If you had the *An Inspector Calls* question from above, a <u>different main idea</u> could be that Sheila's character <u>changes</u> over the course of the play.

*Sandra wished she'd brought a different main outfit.*

## *Hey you — what's the big idea...*

Coming up with a main idea shows the examiner that you've thought about the question. Boy do they love it when you do that. It shows you've used that big thing between your ears, and no... I don't mean your nose...

# Planning — Picking out Your Main Idea

Psst... here's a handy tip.  Use your notes to come up with your main idea.  Keep this to yourself though...

## Each question can be answered with more than one main idea

Sometimes <u>just one</u> main idea won't give you <u>enough</u> to write about — if you can write about <u>more than one</u>, then go for it.  <u>Don't</u> write about <u>too many</u> though — this'll make your answer sound <u>muddled</u>.

*You could write about the techniques Shakespeare uses, such as his use of soliloquies (when characters talk to themselves)...*

*...then how Shakespeare uses the imagery in Macbeth's language to show his thoughts and feelings...*

How does Shakespeare show Macbeth's thoughts and feelings?

*...and then the way in which Macbeth speaks and acts, and how this shows his thoughts and feelings.*

## There are lots of things you can base your main idea on

Here are some <u>examples</u> of things to <u>think about</u> when you're <u>choosing</u> your main idea:

1) The <u>content</u> — what the text is <u>about</u>, or what <u>happens</u> in the text.

2) The <u>language</u> — whether it's formal or informal, descriptive or straight to the point.  Look at what kind of words are used.

3) The <u>mood</u> — whether the writer sounds happy, sad, angry, regretful, etc.  Or think about how the mood makes you feel.

4) <u>Imagery</u> — the writer may have used descriptions to make pictures in your mind when you read them.

5) A <u>hidden meaning</u> — the text could be <u>about</u> something different from what the words actually say.

*These are all good things to make notes on when you're trying to come up with your main idea, but there are other things you could write about.*

Examples:

A <u>hidden meaning</u> idea.

If you had a poem about someone stretching to pick the <u>last</u> apple from a nearly dead tree, your main idea could be that the poem is <u>really</u> about mankind taking too much from the earth, and <u>destroying nature</u>.

Your main idea might be that the <u>language</u> in a <u>play</u> is very <u>emotive</u> because it is trying to get the reader to <u>sympathise</u> with a character.

A <u>language</u> idea.

You might have a main idea about how the writer uses <u>imagery</u> in a novel to make the reader feel like they're <u>actually there</u>.

A <u>mood</u> idea.

An <u>imagery</u> idea.

If you're comparing two war poems, your main idea could be that one is <u>sad</u> about people dying in war, and the other is <u>angry</u> about it.

### Practice Questions

1) What is the main idea in an essay?

2) "You shouldn't have more than one main idea in an essay." — true or false?

3) Name three things you could think about when you're choosing your main idea.

# Example Plans

Right — enough chit-chat, let's get down to business. Here are some pages on what your plans might be like.

## Spider diagrams are a handy way to plan

Look at this question: | How does Priestley present Arthur Birling in *An Inspector Calls*?

1) There are <u>lots</u> of ways to <u>answer</u> this question — so it might be useful to draw a <u>spider diagram</u>.

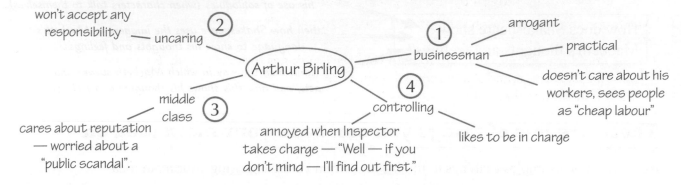

won't accept any
responsibility — uncaring ②

Arthur Birling

arrogant
businessman ① — practical

doesn't care about his
workers, sees people
as "cheap labour"

middle
class ③

controlling ④

likes to be in charge

cares about reputation
— worried about a
"public scandal".

annoyed when Inspector
takes charge — "Well — if you
don't mind — I'll find out first."

2) You can write about <u>each arm</u> of the spider diagram in a <u>separate paragraph</u>. <u>Number</u> the points you're going to make and then write about them <u>one by one</u>.

3) The <u>main idea</u> you focus on could be that Priestley presents Arthur Birling as someone who cares more about his <u>status</u> than <u>other people</u>.

## Lists are useful if you're comparing

| Compare how power is presented in the poems *My Last Duchess* and *Ozymandias*.

1) When you're <u>comparing</u> two texts, look at the <u>similarities</u> and <u>differences</u> between them. You could make a <u>list</u> of points from both texts.

| <u>My Last Duchess</u> | <u>Ozymandias</u> |
|---|---|
| Duke tries to exert power over everyone around him — controls where his companion sits and looks. | Very powerful — repetition in "king of kings" emphasises power over all. |
| Power can be abused — the Duke may have killed his wife — he "gave commands" then "all smiles stopped" (alliteration shows significant event). | "Sneer of cold command" suggests not a benevolent ruler — abused his power. Alliteration shows harshness of rule. |
| Power isn't absolute — broken sentences show confusion over wife's behaviour, e.g. "Somehow — I know not how —" | Power fades with time — narrator says there's "Nothing" left of Ozymandias's "works". |

2) Try to <u>link</u> points together — e.g. both texts use <u>alliteration</u> to demonstrate a character's <u>power</u>.

3) Your <u>main idea</u> could be that both poems show that powerful people can <u>abuse</u> their power, but their power can be affected by the influence of <u>time</u> or certain <u>people</u>.

## *Learn this lot and it'll be plan sailing...*

'Spider-plan' will save the day. He'll swing in, organise your ideas, and then swing back to his home in the cupboard under the stairs. Anyway... there are different ways you can plan your answers, so it's up to you.

# Example Plans

Phew... this is the last page about planning. Remember, plans are all about making your life easier, so you need to decide what kind of plan to use, and if your plan isn't helping you — change it.

## Plans can help you work out what you think

> You are going to enter a journalism competition run by a television magazine. Your entry will be judged by the magazine's editor.
>
> Write a review of a TV show that you have watched.

1) You could use a spider diagram to help you think of things to write about. For this question you could start by thinking about what you liked and disliked about the TV show, and then think of reasons why you liked or disliked those things.

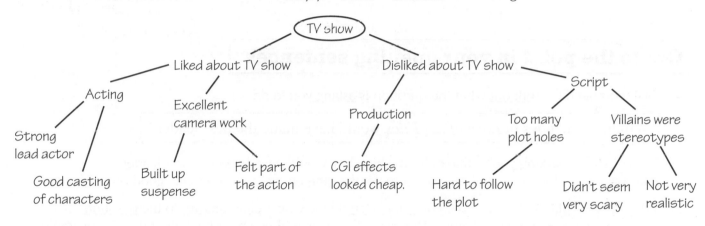

2) Spider diagrams are useful for finding links between your ideas. This can be handy for writing questions, where there are lots of marks available for how you structure your writing.

## Plans are there to help you

1) There's more than one way to plan. Instead of drawing a spider diagram, you could just write a list of your ideas, or lay them out in a table. Work out which type of plan works best for you.

2) The plan is there to help make your writing better. If you think of a really fantastic idea once you've already started writing, you can still put it in as long as it fits in with the rest of the essay.

3) Don't spend all your time planning and no time writing. About 5 minutes should be enough time to write a really top-notch essay plan.

4) Planning is a really good skill to have, so practise writing plans for lots of different questions.

### Practice Questions

1) Give two different ways of planning your essay.

2) "If you're comparing two texts, it's a good idea to link points together in your plan." — true or false?

3) Draw a table to plan an answer to the question 'Write a review of a book you have read recently.'

4) Draw a spider diagram to plan an answer to the question 'Review a film you have watched recently.'

**Section One — The Basics**

# Essay Introductions

You don't need to write detailed introductions for all of your English Language answers, but you'll need to write them for your English Literature essays. These pages will show you how to write a great introduction.

## You need to do three things in your introduction

① <u>Get to the point</u> straight away.

② Make it clear that your answer <u>fits the question</u>.

③ <u>Grab the attention</u> of anyone reading it.

*Make sure the shirt and tie fit the question too.*

## Get to the point in your opening sentences

1) First, you need to <u>work out</u> what the question is <u>asking you</u> to do.

> Which of the boys in *Lord of the Flies* would have made the best leader?

2) The question is <u>asking you</u> to think about <u>which boy</u> would have been the <u>best leader</u>. Plan your essay by thinking about <u>why</u> some of the <u>different boys</u> would make good or bad leaders.

3) When you've <u>planned</u> your essay, you <u>could start</u> it by giving a <u>clear answer</u> to the <u>question</u>. Just give <u>your opinion</u> immediately. The <u>rest</u> of the essay will be about <u>backing it up</u> with <u>examples</u>.

> In 'Lord of the Flies' the boys' survival depends on having a strong leader. Jack and Simon have leadership qualities, but in my opinion it is Ralph who shows himself to be the best leader overall.

*This gets straight to the point and gives an answer to the question.*

4) Or you could give the reader an <u>idea</u> of <u>how</u> you're going to answer the question.

> Several of the boys have features that would have made them a good leader: Piggy's intelligence, Jack's strength, Ralph's common sense and Simon's courage.

*This doesn't give an immediate answer, but it shows you're trying to answer the question. The rest of the essay would be about the strengths and weaknesses of each boy as a possible leader.*

5) Whatever you do, <u>don't</u> just write a <u>load of waffle</u> about what happens in the book.

> In 'Lord of the Flies', a group of boys get stranded on a tropical island. Their plane crashed and the wreckage was washed away. The first two boys we meet are Piggy and Ralph.

*This is all true, but it's not relevant to the question. You don't need to explain everything that's happened.*

## *Sharpen up your introductions — get to the point...*

First impressions are important in essays as well as real life. I once shook hands with someone I'd just met when I had jam on my hand. I never heard from them again. I guess some people just really don't like jam.

# Essay Introductions

Your introduction needs to kick-start your essay — you've got to show the examiner that you're going to answer the question. After all, answered questions are what examiners like the most. Everyone knows that.

## The rest of your introduction gives more detail

1) After you've written your opening sentences showing the examiner that you're going to answer the question, you can give a bit more detail about how you're going to do it.

> How far does Dickens encourage the reader to sympathise with Miss Havisham in *Great Expectations*?

2) Your main idea might be that even though Miss Havisham can be cruel, Dickens wants the reader to feel sympathetic towards her. Your introduction might look something like this:

*This opening sentence tells the examiner your main idea. You're answering the question straight away.*

> Despite her sometimes cruel actions, the reader is readily encouraged to sympathise with Miss Havisham. Dickens presents her as an unhappy and unloved character, and although she treats Pip callously in the novel, the tragic events of her past help to explain her actions. In my opinion, the presentation of Miss Havisham's misery negates her cruelty, suggesting that Dickens wants us to feel sympathy for her overall.

*The next sentence gives some reasons to support your main idea.*

*Here you're giving your opinion on the question.*

## Use the exact question words in your introduction

1) Try to use words or phrases from the question in your first paragraph.

> Explore the idea that *An Inspector Calls* is just an interesting detective story that keeps you guessing.

2) Repeating words from the question will show the examiner that you're answering the question.

> 'An Inspector Calls' keeps you guessing about a variety of things throughout the play, such as why Eva committed suicide and who was responsible for her death. These questions are gradually answered as the play goes on, keeping the reader's attention and making it an interesting detective story. However, the ambiguity at the end of the play surrounding the identity of the Inspector is unusual, and adds interest when compared to a traditional detective story.

3) This will also help you keep the question fresh in your mind so your answer doesn't wander off-topic.

### Practice Questions

1) What do you need to do in the opening line of your essay?
2) What should you aim to do in the first paragraph of your essay?

# Writing Essay Paragraphs

It'd be a shame if you wasted a good introduction by following it with a terrible essay. You need to continue the good work and make a really convincing argument. Remember, use your plan to give you a structure.

## You've got to carry on from the opening paragraph

Write about the points on your plan one by one, keeping each one in a separate paragraph.

> Write about how the relationship between Ralph and Jack changes in *Lord of the Flies*.

The relationship between Ralph and Jack changes dramatically throughout the novel. At the beginning they get on, despite competing to be the leader of the group, but by the end of the novel, Jack is trying to kill Ralph.

*This is the opening paragraph. It puts forward your main idea.*

The relationship between Ralph and Jack falls apart because they have different priorities. Ralph wants to create order on the island and uses the conch shell to call "assemblies". Jack loses interest in an ordered society and becomes obsessed with hunting. They become "unable to communicate" and the tension created by their different priorities causes their relationship to break down.

*This is the first point from your plan. It backs up the main idea.*

*The rest of this paragraph explains your first point using evidence from the novel.*

## You might think of new points that go against your main idea

1) If you realise that you've got lots of great things to say which go against what you've said before, you can still put them into your essay.

2) Just say clearly that you're now writing from the other side of the argument.

When he orders the murder of Macduff's wife and children, Macbeth shows clearly that he is wholly evil.

However, you could argue that Macbeth is not wholly evil, as he only starts to do bad things when other characters persuade him to. At one point, Macbeth decides not to kill Duncan, and he only changes his mind when Lady Macbeth puts pressure on him. This suggests that the good in Macbeth might have stopped him doing evil things, if his wife had not pushed him.

*This sentence makes it clear to the examiner that you're now going to argue from the other side of the argument.*

*Then you've got to carry on. Start by writing about the things you missed out before.*

## *Essay, essay, essay — what 'ave we 'ere then...*

Your plan is only a guide to help you write your essay. If you realise that what you've put in your plan isn't quite right, then don't stick to it blindly. Just make it clear that you've changed your mind and plough on.

**Section One — The Basics**

# Writing Essay Paragraphs

For some questions you might have lots of really good points for both sides of the argument.  If so, you could put it all in your essay, as long as you make it clear in the conclusion what your final decision is.

## You can write an essay looking at both sides of an idea

1) You don't have to <u>choose one perspective</u> and then <u>only</u> write about that side of things.  You can look at <u>both sides</u>.  Remember that you <u>have</u> to give an <u>answer</u> at the end, though (see p.22).

> To what extent does Shakespeare present Romeo as a violent character?

2) You've got <u>two options</u> here.  <u>Either</u> you can make up your mind, or you can argue <u>both sides</u>.  Here's an introduction to an essay arguing <u>both sides</u>.

> At times in 'Romeo and Juliet', Romeo seems like a peaceful character who doesn't like fighting, but he does get involved in a lot of violence, so there are many good reasons to say he is or is not a violent character.  Romeo is not involved in the fighting at the start of the play, and he tries to avoid fighting Tybalt and Paris.  This would suggest that Romeo is not a violent character.  However, when he does fight Tybalt he is like a different person, with "fire eyed fury", and he is quickly provoked to fight Paris.

*This first sentence makes it clear that there are different sides to the argument.*

*Evidence is provided for both sides.  This shows that the essay will look at both why you might think Romeo's violent, and why you might think he isn't.*

> <u>Remember</u> — there isn't <u>one</u> right answer.  It's all about <u>backing up</u> what you say.

## There are a few rules that'll help you write a good essay

Follow these <u>rules</u> when you're writing an answer.

(1) Don't <u>contradict yourself</u>    <u>Don't</u> say <u>one thing</u> in your essay and then say the <u>opposite</u>.  If you think there are <u>two sides</u> to something then explain <u>why</u> and give some <u>evidence</u>.

(2) <u>Stick</u> to the <u>point</u>    <u>Don't</u> get sidetracked — you're <u>not</u> being asked to write down <u>every</u> little thing you know about <u>the text</u>.  Make sure your essay is <u>clear</u> and sticks to the point.

(3) Keep your writing <u>balanced</u> and <u>clear</u>    <u>Don't</u> say <u>rude</u> things like: "Anyone who thinks this is stupid."  Write a <u>balanced</u> essay, using plenty of <u>evidence</u>.

(4) Don't <u>generalise</u>    <u>Don't</u> make <u>sweeping statements</u> like this: "All of Shakespeare's plays get boring in Act IV."  It's <u>too general</u> and you <u>can't</u> back it up.

### Practice Questions

1) What should you write about after your opening paragraph?

2) What should you do if you need to change your argument?

3) What's the best way to argue both sides of an idea in an essay?

# Comparing

Comparing questions are common in English exams, so you need to learn how to answer them.

## Comparing means finding similarities and differences

1) <u>Comparing</u> is all about looking at <u>two or more</u> things <u>together</u>. Look at this question:

> Both of these texts are about the tourism industry.
> Compare the following:
> - the writers' attitudes to the tourism industry
> - how they get across their arguments.

2) For this question, you need to show the <u>similarities</u> and <u>differences</u> between two things:

① the writers' attitudes to the tourism industry

You need to look at what each writer <u>thinks</u> about the tourism industry. You have to make <u>links</u> between attitudes that are <u>similar</u> and attitudes that are <u>different</u>.

② how they get across their arguments.

You need to say whether the <u>techniques</u> the writers use are <u>similar</u> or <u>different</u> in the two texts, along with <u>examples</u> to prove your point.

You must make your comparisons <u>clear</u> — give the <u>similarities</u> and <u>differences</u>, and try to explain <u>why</u> the two things are similar or different.

There weren't many differences between the twins — they <u>both</u> looked ridiculous.

## Link your points together clearly

1) To <u>structure</u> your comparison, you could write a <u>whole paragraph</u> about one text, then a paragraph about the <u>other</u>.

2) Or you could make comparative points about <u>both texts</u> within the <u>same paragraph</u>.

3) However you structure your points, you need to use <u>linking words and phrases</u> to make your comparisons really clear. For example:

> The writer of Item 1 uses negative verbs such as "infested" to suggest that tourism has had a detrimental effect. In contrast, the statistics quoted in Item 2 suggest that the writer of that article has a more positive viewpoint regarding tourism.

*This uses the phrase "in contrast" to link together two different texts in the same paragraph.*

*This paragraph starts with a linking phrase ("on the other hand") to make it clear that it's introducing a comparison with the previous paragraph.*

> In Item 2, on the other hand, the writer presents tourism in a positive light, using evidence from reports to back up her opinions. This makes her seem more trustworthy.

## *Good comedy hosts — they're beyond compère*

Similarities, differences and linking — these are the things to remember when it comes to comparing. Think carefully about how you're structuring your answer — make your points really clear and easy to understand.

**Section One — The Basics**

# Comparing

I love comparing things — take food, for example. I once stood in the supermarket for ten whole minutes comparing the pros and cons of different chocolate bars. I couldn't decide, so I bought strawberries instead.

## You'll have to compare non-fiction texts

1) For English Language, you might get asked a question like this:

> Compare how the two writers convey their different attitudes to teaching.
> In your answer, you could:
> * compare their different attitudes
> * compare the methods they use to convey their attitudes
> * support your ideas with references to both texts.

2) For this question, you need to compare the writer's points of view, as well the techniques they use to get their points across. You might write a point like this:

> The writer of Source A has a strict attitude towards teaching. He uses short sentences, such as "This trend must not continue." These give the text a blunt tone, which shows the writer's strong belief that schools should not be relaxing environments. While Source B's writer uses similar techniques, her viewpoint is very different. Her use of multiple short sentences gives the text a fast, exciting pace. This reflects her enthusiasm for "relaxed" methods of teaching, which she sees as more effective than the strict teaching style that Source A's writer prefers.

*This answer compares the writers' attitudes and the techniques they use.*

## You might also have to compare poems

1) For English Literature, you might get a question like this:

> Compare how language is used in *The Manhunt* and one other poem.

2) You've got to write about the poem in the question and compare it to another poem you've chosen. One of your points could be something like this:

> The poets in 'The Manhunt' and 'Valentine' both use imagery that does not match what is described. In 'The Manhunt' the shrapnel inside the woman's husband is described as "a foetus of metal". This image of a baby contrasts with the horror of his injuries. In 'Valentine', an onion is portrayed as a romantic object, and described as a "moon wrapped in brown paper". The images in both poems are at odds with what they are describing, which makes them stand out more to the reader.

*This answer talks about both of the poems together.*

### Practice Questions

1) What should you use to link your points together in comparing questions?

2) Choose two poems you're studying. Write an essay comparing the way that both poets use language to present their ideas to the reader. Use P.E.E.D. to support your argument.

**Section One — The Basics**

# Writing About Text Extracts

On this page, there's a bit of info about what to expect in your English Language exams. The next few pages will then walk you through some example questions and the fiction and non-fiction texts they're about.

## Read the extracts carefully

1) For your English Language exams, you'll have to answer <u>questions</u> about at least one <u>fiction</u> text — either a <u>short story</u> or an <u>extract</u> from a story.

2) You'll also need to answer questions about two <u>non-fiction</u> texts — these could include things like <u>newspaper</u>, <u>magazine</u> or <u>website articles</u>, <u>travel writing</u> or <u>biographies</u>.

3) You <u>won't</u> get to study these texts in class — the <u>first time</u> you'll see them is in the exams.

4) At the start of each exam, spend <u>10 to 15 minutes</u> reading through the questions and extracts. As you read, you could <u>underline</u> key words, phrases and techniques that will help you <u>answer the questions</u>.

## You'll have to tackle different types of questions

1) Some of the questions you'll be asked will be about <u>finding information</u>. You could be asked to simply <u>list</u> some <u>facts</u>, or you might be asked to <u>explain</u> what you've <u>learnt</u> from a text.

2) In the non-fiction paper, you'll have to <u>summarise</u> something in your <u>own words</u> — to do this you'll need to take ideas from <u>two</u> texts.

3) You'll also have to explain <u>how</u> the writer of a text <u>achieves</u> certain effects or <u>influences</u> the reader, e.g. how they try to <u>persuade</u> their audience to do something.

- You could be asked about the effects of the <u>language</u> in a text, e.g. the writer's <u>choice</u> of <u>words</u>, and the <u>tone</u> they've created.

- You might also have to write about the effect that the text's <u>structure</u> (the way the writer <u>organises</u> their ideas) has on the reader.

4) You'll have to <u>compare</u> two texts, i.e. look at the <u>similarities</u> and <u>differences</u> between them. You'll usually have to compare the two writers' <u>points of view</u> about something <u>specific</u>, as well as <u>how</u> they convey their points of view.

5) You'll also need to evaluate how <u>successful</u> a writer is at <u>achieving</u> something in the text, e.g. creating a particular <u>mood</u> or making characters seem <u>realistic</u>.

## You need to write clear, organised answers

1) Unless the question asks you to write your answer as a list, you should always write your answers in <u>paragraphs</u>. Start a <u>new paragraph</u> for every new point you make, and use <u>linking words</u> (see p.9) to make your writing really <u>organised</u> and <u>clear</u>.

2) You should use <u>P.E.E.D.</u> (see pages 4-5) to make sure your points are <u>well-structured</u> and clearly <u>answer the question</u>.

---

### *That exam text was so boring — a really vanilla extract...*

Bear in mind that fiction texts in English Language exams will often be extracts from a longer text, such as a novel or short story. Make sure you don't go writing about extracts as if they're whole texts by themselves.

# Example Fiction Extract

Read this extract from a novel — it's the kind of thing you'll have to read for the fiction part of your English Language exams. Then have a look at the example questions and answers below and on page 28.

The story of my life can be split quite clearly into three parts.

The third era, today's era, is a happy one. I may not lead a particularly exciting life these days, but as I get older it's the simple things that please — the quiet rustle of the morning newspaper; the joy of spring's first green shoots in the garden.

The first era was happy too: a childhood spent tumbling through golden fields of corn; the sound of laughter ringing in my ears; my juvenile fingers and tongue stained with the juice of the ripe, tangy blackberries that grew in the hedges along the lane.

And as for the second era… well, you'll see.

I left the countryside in 1979, when I was offered a job as a planning assistant for a company that redeveloped old properties, especially high-rise buildings. I'd never even seen a building that tall, let alone been involved in rebuilding one, but nevertheless I packed my bags and bought a one-way bus ticket.

Everything went well until June of that year, when the company acquired the Brunnings mansion. It was a lonely old place built of coal-dark stone, with huge wooden doors that reminded me of tombstones. Looking back, there was always something strange about it. Even at night it was never silent. Instead there was the constant moan of the wind, the groan of restless floorboards, the incessant creak of doors as they swung on their hinges. We heard rumours about some kind of ancient curse, too, but we brushed them aside, too occupied by congratulatory champagne and our excitement over the plans we were making.

No, I didn't think anything of the rumours then, but looking back, if I'd known what would happen — how close I would come to losing everything — I'd have caught the first bus back to the countryside...

## You'll have to write about the effect of language

How does the writer use language to describe the narrator's life?

You could include the writer's choice of:
* words and phrases
* language features and techniques
* sentence forms.

*For this question, you only need to write about language techniques.*

*Try to cover all the bullet points in your answer.*

*Make a clear point at the beginning of each paragraph — remember P.E.E.D.*

*Always write about the effect of the writer's language.*

The writer uses sensory descriptions to describe the narrator's life. She refers to the "sound of laughter" and describes the taste of the "tangy" blackberries. This appeal to the senses makes the reader imagine similar experiences of their own, which helps them to build a strong, detailed picture of what the narrator's life is like.

# Fiction Extract Questions

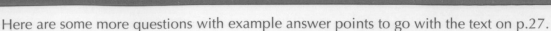

Here are some more questions with example answer points to go with the text on p.27.

## You'll need to write about the text's structure

How has the writer structured the text to gain and hold the reader's interest?

You could write about:

- what the writer focuses your attention on at the beginning
- how and why the writer changes this focus as the extract develops
- any other structural features that interest you.

*All your points need to be about the text's structure.*

*You need to write about the whole extract in your answer.*

*Using technical terms like this will impress the examiner.*

*Always link your answers back to the question — you need to explain why your example makes the text more interesting.*

The writer gains the reader's interest by using a non-linear narrative, in which the narrator talks initially about the present, then about different periods from her past. This structure allows the writer to hint that something bad has happened in the narrator's life, including the idea that she came "close" to "losing everything". This is interesting for the reader because they are held in suspense as to what happened, and would want to read on to find out more.

## You'll also have to evaluate the text

"The writer vividly describes the atmosphere of the Brunnings mansion. The reader can really imagine what it is like there."

To what extent do you agree?

In your response, you could:

- write about your own feelings on reading the passage
- evaluate how the writer has created those feelings
- support your opinions with references to the text.

*This question gives you a statement — you need to evaluate how far you agree with what it's saying.*

*Always back up your opinion by explaining how the writer has affected the reader.*

I strongly agree that the atmosphere of the Brunnings mansion is vividly described. This is partly achieved by the writer's use of onomatopoeia when describing the mansion. For example, she describes the "groan" of the floorboards. By mimicking the noises of the house, the writer gives the reader the same experience as the main character, so they would feel the haunting atmosphere too.

*Give your opinion on the statement in the question.*

*It's great to embed short quotes into your sentences as evidence to back up your points.*

*You need to explain how your evidence proves your point.*

## Make sure you know what to write about...

You might get an English Language question in which you have to write about both structure <u>and</u> language. Make sure you know exactly what you need to cover in your answer before you start writing anything.

# Example Non-Fiction Texts

Read both of these non-fiction texts — there are some example questions and answers on page 30.

## Item 1

# INSECTS FOR HEALTH
### The new trend in healthy eating

It's the health food sensation that's sweeping the nation, with celebrities and nutritionists alike raving wildly about the benefits. But can eating insects really be as beneficial to your health as food experts claim?

### Nutritionally balanced
The short answer is yes — and the science proves it. As well as being surprisingly tasty, insects are a highly nutritious alternative to meat and fish.

> **Insects:**
> - are high in fibre
> - are high in protein
> - contain all the minerals found in other meats
> - retain vitamins through the cooking process

### A cultivated food source
Insect farms have been scientifically developed to offer a hygienic and disease-free food source. The latest insect-farming methods also provide a sustainable supply of food, unlike traditional livestock.

Farmed insects are fed an exclusively vegetarian diet. They eat only nutritious herbs and grasses, which are said to improve the flavour even further.

### Cooking with insects
Insects can be used as a replacement for meat in most meals. Experts recommend crickets, grasshoppers or ants as particularly good substitutes for traditional meat products.

Insects are naturally more tender, so need less time to cook than other meats. They are particularly tasty dry-fried or grilled, so you can use less fat overall in your cooking.

### Easier to buy than ever
Nowadays, you'll find insects in the freezer department of all major supermarkets. They are often fully prepared for cooking, which saves time and effort for busy families.

### 'Novelty' food
Some dismiss insect eating as a fad which will die down once the initial novelty wears off.

But with the golden combination of health benefits, ethical sustainability and convenience, we think insect eating could be one trend that's here to stay.

## Item 2

# The insect craze that's difficult to swallow

**Ed Lewis**

Farmers and landowners staged a rally at Westminster yesterday, protesting against the current craze for eating insects. They claim that sales of insects are damaging the profitability of traditional meat farms, putting them at risk of closure.

I can see why they have concerns. As the trend for eating insects gains momentum among health food fanatics, supermarkets have seen obsessive fans flocking to stores to get their hands on frozen insects — and every penny that's spent on an insect-based meal is a penny lost for traditional meat farmers.

It's true that insects can be healthier and easier to cook than regular meat — but does that matter so much, when

the livelihoods of UK meat farmers are being rapidly destroyed?

A statement issued by the Farm Owners' Association suggests that the insect trend is responsible for a 17% fall in sales of conventional meats through domestic channels since June.

This simply cannot go on. The financial implications for our British farmers, many of whom are already struggling, will be dire unless the government takes prompt action.

Farmers are also concerned over the rising number of amateur insect hunters who trespass onto private farmland, inspired by the food they see on sale in the supermarkets. Insect hunters leave gates open, trample crops and leave unsightly litter behind. This destruction of property is appalling — and illegal.

The FOA are rightly insisting on a total ban of all insect sales in supermarkets. The government must listen to their concerns, and act fast to avoid further damage to the fragile agricultural economy in this country. Without a ban, the UK meat industry may never recover.

# Non-Fiction Text Questions

Have a look at these example questions and answers, which are about the non-fiction texts on page 29.

## You'll have to analyse how extracts are written

*You need to think about the way this text is written.*

Read Item 2.
How does the writer use language to persuade readers that the trend for eating insects is a bad thing?

*You need to say how the writer tries to convince the reader. For more on persuasive language, see pages 44-47.*

In Item 2, the writer persuades the reader through their choice of strong negative verbs such as "damaging" and "destroyed". These verbs give the reader the impression that the trend for eating insects is a bad thing, so they would be more likely to agree with the writer that selling insects should be banned.

*Give examples of specific words that the writer uses to make their argument more convincing.*

*Explain the effect that the writer's language has on the reader.*

## Sometimes you'll need to summarise two texts

*You need to write a summary — explain the advantages using material from both texts.*

Look at Item 1 and Item 2.
Summarise the advantages of eating insects.

*This question asks you to give examples from both sources.*

*For summaries, you don't need to compare the two texts, but you do need to give evidence from them both.*

Both sources suggest that insects are a healthy alternative to traditional meat products. Item 1 says they're a "nutritious alternative", and Item 2 says they can be "healthier... than regular meat." The two texts also state that...

*To write a good summary, you need to cover all the main ideas in both texts.*

## You'll also have to compare two texts

*For more on comparing see p.24-25.*

Look again at Item 1 and Item 2.
Compare how the two writers convey their different attitudes to eating insects. Write about:
* what the writers say about eating insects
* how they convey their views to the reader.

*You need to pick out the similarities and differences between the writers' views on eating insects.*

*You also need to look for similarities and differences between the techniques that the writers use.*

The writer of Item 1 has a positive attitude towards the insect eating trend, whereas in Item 2 a more negative point of view is expressed. In Item 1, the writer says that "crickets, grasshoppers or ants" are all good meat substitutes. The list of three highlights that they are a flexible and abundant food source, which demonstrates the writer's belief that insect eating is "here to stay". Item 2 also uses a list of three in the penultimate paragraph, but the writer uses it to convey a different opinion to the writer in Item 1: the list suggests that there are a large number of negative consequences to insect hunting. This builds on the impression that the overall influence of insect eating is harmful.

*You need to write about both texts in your answer.*

*Make sure you cover the writers' attitudes, and the techniques they use.*

# Writing About Novels and Plays

For your English Literature exams, you'll have studied whole novels and plays in advance. You'll be asked to write some long essays about the texts you've studied, so you'll need to have a really good grip on them.

## Know the novel or the play that you're studying

1) To be able to answer the questions in the exam, you'll need to know the book or the play that you're studying really well.

2) Carefully read the questions you're going to answer a few times, and think about the key characters, events and themes that you'll need to write about.

## Some questions are about one character

*This question is asking you how a character has changed during the novel.*

How is Ralph changed by his experiences on the island in *Lord of the Flies*? Remember to refer to:
- what he does
- how the events make him feel
- the methods used by the writer to present these events.

*Think about Ralph's reaction to the events.*

*This point is asking you about the writer. Don't leave that part out when you answer the question.*

## Some are about themes in the text

*This is a question about a specific theme — social class.*

*You have to refer to the way several characters talk about social class.*

How does the writer explore ideas about social class in *Blood Brothers*? Remember to refer to:
- what different characters in the play think about social class
- how the writer presents social class.

*You need to write about the techniques the writer uses to explore social class.*

## Questions can ask about the style or effect

This question asks about the style of a play — what it's like — and the effect it has on the audience.

How is suspense created in *An Inspector Calls*? Remember to refer to:
- what the Inspector says and does
- how the other characters respond to the Inspector
- the way Priestley presents the Inspector.

*Plays are often shorter than novels, so every word counts. Think about the effect of the language used by each character, and why the author has used those words.*

*Plays are written to be performed in front of an audience, so think about the stage directions and how the play might look on stage.*

## Practice Question

1) Choose a theme from one of the texts you have studied. Find five examples in the text that you think deal with that theme. Write a sentence about each quote to explain what it shows about the theme.

Section Two — Writing About Texts

# Planning Your Literature Essay

For your English Literature exams, you'll need to plan out each essay before you write it.
Have a look at the example plan on this page to see how it's done.

## Don't forget the bullet points when you plan

Some questions will have <u>bullet points</u> to help you <u>make sense</u> of the <u>question</u>.

> How does Dickens explore the theme of
> social responsibility in *A Christmas Carol*?
> Remember to refer to:
> * what the characters say and do
> * how Dickens conveys his views.

*Use the bullet points
from the question to
help make your plan.*

*Always have a Plan Bee.*

## Put some examples with the notes in your plan

*For more on planning
see p.12-17.*

The <u>secret</u> of planning literature essays is <u>finding details</u> from the text that <u>back up</u> your answer.
The examples you find need to be <u>relevant</u>, otherwise your essay <u>won't</u> answer the question.

> Scrooge is dismissive of the poor to begin with — he calls them
> "surplus population" and refuses to donate money to help them.
>
> Scrooge changes — he donates money to the charity collectors.
> He becomes much happier — he has a "delighted smile".
>
> Ignorance and Want are described as "Man's" children, i.e. our responsibility. They're
> described using adjectives such as "ragged" and "wretched" — they've been badly neglected.

## Use your examples to support your points

Use the <u>examples</u> you've found to <u>plan</u> the <u>points</u> you want to make in your essay.
You can <u>number</u> your <u>points</u> in the <u>order</u> you want to write about them.

> 1) Dickens suggests it's morally wrong to not be socially responsible. Scrooge
>    isn't socially responsible to begin with — calls poor people "surplus population".
>    He's also described as a "sinner" — suggests his attitude to the poor is wrong.
>
> 2) Dickens shows that being socially responsible brings happiness / fulfilment.
>    When Scrooge has learnt social responsibility (e.g. makes a large
>    donation to a charity) he's much happier — he has a "delighted smile".
>
> 3) Dickens shows that ignoring social responsibility has horrific effects on
>    society. Ignorance and Want — "Man's" neglect of them has left them
>    "wretched" — shows the consequences of ignoring responsibility to others.

*Use your
examples to
support the
points you want
to make.*

*Remember, your
points have
to respond to
the question.*

## *Questions from the left — no right answers...*

Lots of English questions don't have one right answer — it's all about backing up your case with evidence.
Make sure that for every point you make, you include a relevant, clearly-explained example from the text.

# Writing Your Literature Essay

If you're going to set out your points clearly, you've got to use your plan. It'll help you make sure you get all your important ideas in, and it'll give your essay a proper structure.

## Follow your plan and link your points together

Your plan should give you all the key information you need for your answer.

How do the characters in *An Inspector Calls* change over the course of the play? Write about:
- characters whose attitudes change
- characters whose attitudes stay the same.

*For this question you need to think about several different characters. You could compare how they change over the course of the play, and speculate why that might be.*

Plan
- Mr Birling doesn't change — he wants to continue as normal, believing that it's "All over" at the end of the play.
- Sheila is changed by the Inspector — argues with her parents and refuses to put Gerald's engagement ring back on.
- Eric also changes — Inspector's words frighten him. Split between generations.

*Your plan will include the main points you want to write about. Make sure all your points answer the question.*

Whilst all the characters are somewhat affected by the Inspector's words, not all of the characters change by the end of the play. For example, Mr Birling doesn't change at all — he says that the Inspector gave him a "scare", but that it's "All over now." This shows that he hasn't taken in the Inspector's message about his selfish behaviour, and still hasn't understood that he acted wrongly in firing Eva Smith.

In contrast, Sheila is strongly affected by...

*Every time you start a new point, start a new paragraph — it makes your argument clearer.*

## Back up your answer with P.E.E.D.

*See p.4-5 for more on P.E.E.D.*

None of the questions you're asked will have just one right answer, but that doesn't mean you can write anything. You have to make sure your essay's made up of points that you can back up with examples.

How do Juliet's feelings towards her family change in *Romeo and Juliet*?

*There isn't one right answer to a question like this. The examiner will give you marks for how well you support your argument.*

After Juliet gets married, her feelings about her family become confused, as she's torn between her family and Romeo. This is shown in Act III, Scene ii, when she finds out that Romeo has killed Tybalt. Juliet is upset that Romeo killed Tybalt, but she defends Romeo's actions by saying that Tybalt "would have slain" him. This shows that Juliet's feelings towards her family are changing. Earlier in the play Juliet is mainly controlled by her family, but here she shows that her feelings for Romeo are more important.

*This point needs examples to support it.*

*This example supports the point.*

*This explains how your example supports your point.*

*This develops the point by linking it back to the question.*

## Practice Questions

1) How can you support the points you make in a literature essay?
2) When you're writing an essay, what should you do when you want to make a new point?

# Writing About Poems

It's not just novels and plays you'll have to write about for English Literature — it's also jolly old poems too. You'll need a good knowledge of all the poems you're studying — you'll be asked to compare two of them.

## You might be asked about one poem

Write about the poem *Ozymandias* and its effect on you.
Remember to refer to:
* the mood and atmosphere
* the structure and style
* your reaction to the poem.

*The question is asking for your opinion on the poem.*

1) To answer this kind of question you need to think about how the poem makes you feel.

2) Think about how the poet has used language, structure and form to make you react in a certain way.

3) Write down any words, phrases or images that stick in your head and think about why they are memorable.

## You'll definitely need to compare poems

Comparing means talking about the similarities and the differences between things.

Compare the way that places are presented in
*The Prelude: Stealing the Boat* and one other poem.
Remember to refer to:
* what the poems are about and how they are organised
* how the poets create effects in the poems
* the poems' contexts.

*Look for similarities and differences in the way each poem describes a place.*

*Look for examples of the things these bullet points ask for in each poem. Then you can look at the similarities and differences between the examples from each poem.*

1) To answer this kind of question you need to spot the similarities and differences between the two poems. Use the bullet points to help you find them.

2) Think about why the poets have chosen similar or different language and techniques to present places.

3) Don't forget to give your own interpretation of the poems. Think about whether the poets are successful in presenting different places and give reasons why you think that, backed up with evidence from the poems.

There's more about comparing poems on pages 36-37.

## *Throw your anthology out the window — it's poetry in motion...*

You have to read poems very carefully, especially the bits with imagery in. If the imagery isn't clear the first time you read it, then read it again. Think about why the poet's used that imagery and how it makes you feel.

# Poetry Questions

Watch out — you need to give lots of detail when you're writing poetry essays. Poems are usually shorter than plays or novels, so the examiners need a really in-depth analysis of the techniques the poets use.

## You need to read the question carefully

What effect does *London* by William Blake have on you? Remember to refer to:
* the poet's use of words and images
* the tone or mood of the poem.

*Pick out any interesting images and think about why the poet has chosen to use them.*

*To work out the tone or mood of the poem, look for words or images that show whether the poem is happy, sad, regretful, light, dark etc.*

## You also need to read the poem carefully

Read the poem <u>carefully</u>, picking out <u>details</u> and <u>examples</u> to help you <u>answer</u> the <u>question</u>.

London

I wander through each chartered street,
Near where the chartered Thames does flow,
And mark in every face I meet
Marks of weakness, marks of woe.

In every cry of every man,
In every infant's cry of fear,
In every voice, in every ban,
The mind-forged manacles I hear.

How the chimney-sweeper's cry
Every black'ning church appals,
And the hapless soldier's sigh
Runs in blood down palace walls.

But most through midnight streets I hear
How the youthful harlot's curse
Blasts the new-born infant's tear,
And blights with plagues the marriage hearse.

William Blake

*The word "chartered", meaning 'mapped out or legally defined', is repeated, which makes London feel restrictive and confined.*

*The poem uses lots of sensory words, like "cry", which appeal to the reader's sense of hearing.*

*The alliteration in "mind-forged manacles" (handcuffs) draws our attention to the idea that people are trapped by their own thoughts and attitudes.*

*The poet suggests that ordinary people suffer, but those in the "palace" are protected by "walls".*

*The "marriage hearse" is an oxymoron — it suggests that even happy things like marriage are corrupted by the city.*

When you've picked out some <u>details</u> and <u>examples</u>, <u>arrange</u> your <u>evidence</u> in a <u>plan</u>:

1) Reader feels sympathy towards Londoners because of their hard circumstances — they "cry" and "sigh", showing emotional distress.

2) Less sympathetic because of "mind-forged manacles" — own fault?

3) Mention of the "palace walls" hints at who's ultimately to blame — restores sympathy for ordinary people.

Main idea — The poem overall has a sympathetic effect on the reader.

## Practice Questions

1) Find two poems on a similar theme. Write down five ways that the poems are similar or different.

2) "You should never plan your poetry essays." — true or false?

# Comparing Poems

You've had a look at a question on one poem — now look at this question on two poems. Comparing two poems is tricky, but you've got these pages to help you out — and you can flick back to page 34 too.

## First look at what the question's asking

Compare how the poets present their feelings about London in *London* and *Composed Upon Westminster Bridge*. Remember to refer to:
* the poets' feelings about London
* how the poets' feelings are shown in the way they write about London.

*'London' is on p.35 and 'Composed Upon Westminster Bridge' is on p.38.*

1) This question's asking you <u>how</u> the poets show their <u>feelings</u> about <u>London</u>. Look for <u>similarities</u> and <u>differences</u> in the way they write about London.

2) Look at the <u>imagery</u> they use and any <u>techniques</u> (like rhyme or alliteration) to find any <u>similarities</u> or <u>differences</u> between the poems.

## Look for similarities and differences

1) Make some <u>notes</u> on the things that might show the <u>poets' feelings</u> about <u>London</u>.

2) Then you can use the notes to look for <u>similarities</u> and <u>differences</u> between them.

London

1) Short poem. Doesn't tell a story — just the poet walking around London.

2) Poet describes the city with a series of images of ordinary people — creates a list effect.

3) Feelings not directly explained, but made clear through use of negative language.

4) The Thames is described as "chartered". Makes the city seem restrictive.

Composed Upon Westminster Bridge

1) Short poem. Doesn't tell a story — just the poet looking at London.

2) Poet describes the city with lists "Ships, towers, domes, theatres".

3) Poet describes reaction to the city — it's "touching in its majesty" and you'd have to be "Dull... of soul" not to be impressed by it.

4) The Thames glides at its "own sweet will" — it's peaceful and undisturbed.

Think of a <u>main idea</u> (see p.14-15) that you want to focus your essay on. For example, you could talk about how the poets present their <u>feelings</u> about London <u>differently</u>. Blake uses a series of <u>images</u> to give the impression that he feels London is a <u>miserable</u> place. Wordsworth <u>lists</u> what he sees and tells the reader how the city's beauty makes him <u>feel</u>.

## *Let's swap poems — I need a change of image...*

Remember — to compare the two poems, you've got to write about their similarities and differences. Use phrases like 'In comparison', 'On the other hand', 'Similarly' and 'In contrast' to link your points.

# Comparing Poems

When you've finished your planning, you can do some actual writing.

## Keep the poems linked together

Start by making a <u>clear point</u> about something from <u>both poems</u>.
If you <u>link</u> the two poems together, it shows the examiner that you're <u>comparing them</u>.

> Wordsworth clearly describes how he feels about the city, but Blake is less direct. Wordsworth says you would have to be "Dull... of soul" to not be impressed by the city, and that he "never felt, a calm so deep!". In contrast, Blake does not say what his feelings are, but he describes what he sees and hears, such as the "cry" of "infants". Wordsworth conveys his feelings to the reader by describing exactly what they are, whereas Blake uses imagery to show the reader what London is like, which helps them to understand his negative feelings about the city.

*Look for ways to link the poems together. This sentence shows you're considering both poems.*

## Quote examples and link them

Give some <u>examples</u> to <u>support</u> your <u>points</u>.

*Start by making a point about both poems.*

*Use accurate quotes to support your points.*

*Using technical terms like "cumulative effect" will impress the examiner.*

> Blake and Wordsworth use similar techniques to present their different feelings about London. Blake lists a series of images of "woe", which create a cumulative effect of misery, emphasised by the repetition of the phrase "In every". These techniques highlight the magnitude of the suffering that Blake witnesses in London.

> Wordsworth also uses lists to describe what he sees: "Ships, towers, domes, theatres, and temples". This presents the features of London in quick succession, which suggests that the city is a very large place. This helps to convey a sense of London's grandeur to the reader.

*Words like this show that you're writing about both poems together.*

*Explain what your evidence shows.*

*Quote plenty of egg-samples.*

## Your writing must be interesting and clear

Examiners give <u>good marks</u> to people who <u>write clearly</u> and <u>use interesting phrases</u>.

> Wordsworth's description of London makes it feel like a very peaceful place. He describes the Thames as it "glideth" at its "own sweet will" which suggests the river is calm and undisturbed. This calmness is echoed in the houses, which are personified as "asleep". Blake's description, on the other hand...

*If you can use impressive words like "echoed" and "personified" accurately, then you will impress the examiner.*

*Remember, you need to write about both poems.*

# Planning Your Poetry Essay

Now you get to see how to put an essay together from the beginning. It's pretty exciting stuff.

## Look closely at the question

In *Composed Upon Westminster Bridge*, how does Wordsworth use language to present his ideas about the city? Remember to refer to:
* Wordsworth's use of words and images
* the ideas in the poem.

*Think about what ideas are presented in the poem and why they have been chosen.*

*Think about how the poet uses particular words and images to put across his ideas about the city.*

Find examples of <u>images</u>, <u>language</u>, <u>poetic techniques</u> etc. in the poem that show <u>Wordsworth's thoughts</u> about the <u>city</u>.

Composed Upon Westminster Bridge

Earth has not anything to show more fair:
Dull would he be of soul who could pass by
A sight so touching in its majesty:
This City now doth, like a garment, wear
The beauty of the morning; silent, bare,
Ships, towers, domes, theatres, and temples lie
Open unto the fields, and to the sky;
All bright and glittering in the smokeless air.
Never did sun more beautifully steep
In his first splendour, valley, rock or hill;
Ne'er saw I, never felt, a calm so deep!
The river glideth at his own sweet will:
Dear God! the very houses seem asleep;
And all that mighty heart is lying still!

William Wordsworth

## You could plan using a spider diagram

Go through the poem and note down ideas in a <u>spider diagram</u>.

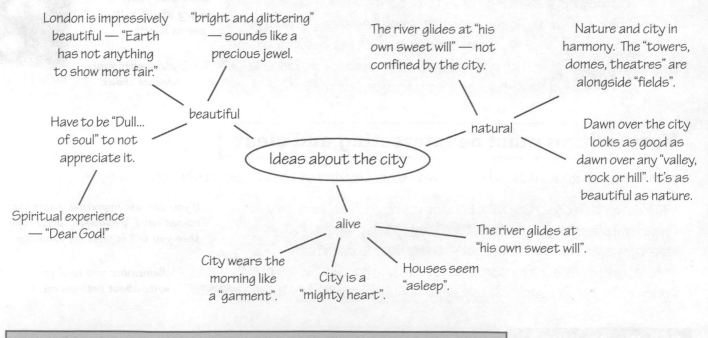

You could pick out a <u>main idea</u> from your <u>spider diagram</u> which you can <u>focus</u> your essay on. In this plan the main idea could be that Wordsworth uses <u>beautiful</u> and <u>natural images</u> to make the city seem <u>alive</u> and <u>impressive</u>.

**Section Two — Writing About Texts**

# Worked Answer

This page will give you some ideas on how to answer the poetry question on p.38. You lucky devils.

## Start off with a cracking introduction

A good introduction will show the examiner the <u>main things</u> you'll <u>talk about</u> in your <u>essay</u>.

*Giving a little bit of an explanation about the poem shows that you've understood it.*

*This shows you're thinking about the question — how the poet uses language to show his ideas about the city.*

> Wordsworth's poem is about the beautiful sights he sees from Westminster Bridge at dawn. An important feature of the poem is how Wordsworth uses beautiful and natural images so that the city seems impressive and alive.

*This is the main idea of the essay, so it should go first.*

## Support your ideas with evidence

Make sure every point is supported with <u>evidence</u>. Here's an <u>example</u>.

*This is a point about personification.*

*Explain why the evidence supports the point.*

> Wordsworth uses personification to make London seem alive and more than just a city. He talks about the city wearing the "beauty of the morning" like a "garment" and that it is like a "mighty heart". By giving the city human characteristics, Wordsworth makes it seem more impressive than a collection of buildings.

*Support your points with quotes from the poem.*

Here's another example:

*This is introducing a point about the imagery in the poem.*

*This evidence backs up the point.*

> Wordsworth uses imagery to make the city seem beautiful. He says that the city at dawn is "bright and glittering" which makes you think that the city is like a precious jewel. This image makes the city seem almost supernatural in its beauty, which helps to convey the strength of Wordsworth's feelings to the reader.

*Round off your point by linking back to the question.*

## Finish off with a strong conclusion

Use your conclusion to <u>answer</u> the <u>question</u> and <u>highlight</u> the <u>main idea</u> of your <u>essay</u>.

*Put your main idea first.*

> The language that Wordsworth uses is chosen to make the city seem very special and more than just a collection of buildings. The poem's language, especially its personification and beautiful imagery, clearly presents Wordsworth's idea that the city is impressive and alive.

*Give an answer to the question.*

# Writing Non-Fiction

These pages are all about how to write articles, letters, speeches, leaflets and reviews. The tricky thing is that you've got to change your writing style to suit whatever it is you're writing and who you're writing for.

## The style of an article should fit the situation

This is where it gets <u>tricky</u>. You're being <u>marked</u> on two things here — how well you <u>answer</u> the question, and how well you write in the <u>style</u> of a <u>real article</u>.

> Write an article for your school newspaper persuading your school to support a charity.

*You need to write in a punchy style, like a newspaper.*

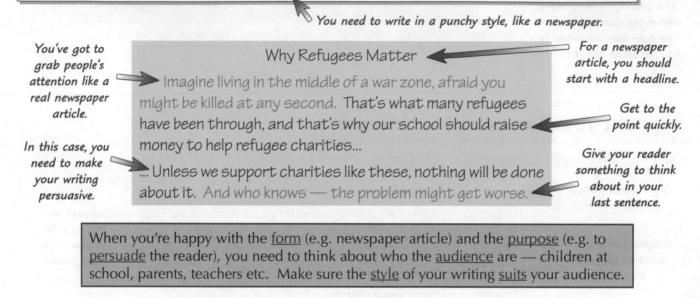

*You've got to grab people's attention like a real newspaper article.*

*In this case, you need to make your writing persuasive.*

### Why Refugees Matter

Imagine living in the middle of a war zone, afraid you might be killed at any second. That's what many refugees have been through, and that's why our school should raise money to help refugee charities...

... Unless we support charities like these, nothing will be done about it. And who knows — the problem might get worse.

*For a newspaper article, you should start with a headline.*

*Get to the point quickly.*

*Give your reader something to think about in your last sentence.*

When you're happy with the <u>form</u> (e.g. newspaper article) and the <u>purpose</u> (e.g. to <u>persuade</u> the reader), you need to think about who the <u>audience</u> are — children at school, parents, teachers etc. Make sure the <u>style</u> of your writing <u>suits</u> your audience.

## The tone of a letter depends on who you're writing to

*Here you've got to write a formal letter, using clear formal language.*

> Write a letter to the headteacher in favour of keeping school meals.

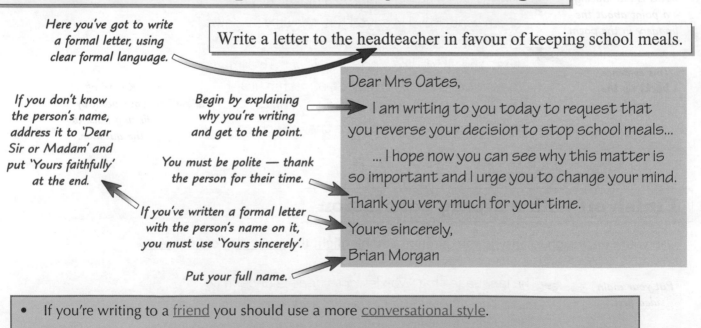

*If you don't know the person's name, address it to 'Dear Sir or Madam' and put 'Yours faithfully' at the end.*

*Begin by explaining why you're writing and get to the point.*

*You must be polite — thank the person for their time.*

*If you've written a formal letter with the person's name on it, you must use 'Yours sincerely'.*

*Put your full name.*

Dear Mrs Oates,

  I am writing to you today to request that you reverse your decision to stop school meals...

  ... I hope now you can see why this matter is so important and I urge you to change your mind.

Thank you very much for your time.

Yours sincerely,

Brian Morgan

- If you're writing to a <u>friend</u> you should use a more <u>conversational style</u>.

- You can start by writing "<u>Dear Paul</u>" — instead of giving the person's title and their last name.

- At the end you could write something like "<u>Take care</u>" rather than "Yours sincerely".

# Writing Non-Fiction

Ah... some more questions. Well, it's all for the good, so keep 'em coming.

## Speeches are usually quite formal

Speeches are often <u>polite</u> and <u>formal</u>, especially when they're addressed to people you <u>don't know</u>. However, you can make them <u>more conversational</u> and <u>humorous</u> if you're talking to people you do <u>know</u>.

> Write a speech for your class with the title 'Smartphones: a luxury or a necessity?'

*This is a speech addressed to your class, so you can use a more friendly tone and some humour.*

*Address your audience at the start. If you're talking to strangers then you could begin with 'Ladies and Gentlemen' and introduce yourself.*

*Think of a polite way of ending your speech.*

Good morning,

I stand here before you as a self-confessed smartphone addict. I can't go 5 minutes without checking my newsfeed, updating my status or sending a message...

... A smartphone may be a luxury, but for me it has become a necessity. I can't live without my smartphone, and I'm sure most of you can't either.

Thank you for listening.

*Use examples to support what you're saying.*

## Leaflets are often about getting the reader to agree with you

> Write a leaflet to persuade people to have their summer holiday in Britain.

*You should have a heading to capture the reader's attention.*

*Think of a way to appeal to the reader — this is an example of using descriptive language.*

*Leaflets often also need to provide information.*

Cor Blighty!

Picture yourself on a quiet English river, a fishing rod in one hand and a cool drink in the other. Imagine your eyes half-closed, the smell of cut grass in the air and the sound of warbling birds all around.

Why pay a small fortune to travel somewhere not as good as Britain?

For only £50 you can book a holiday in...

*Using rhetorical questions is a clever way of persuading a reader to agree with you. See p.44.*

## You need to give your opinion in a review

> Write a review of a film you have watched.

*In this question, you need to decide who you're writing for, e.g. school newsletter, newspaper, magazine. The tone of your review should suit your readers.*

A Comedy of Errors

Ted Austin's latest, so-called comedy is a triumph of poor humour, terrible acting and shoddy editing.

'To Baku and Back' is a film that tries too hard to be funny, but never succeeds in raising a smile...

... Do not waste your money, avoid this film!

*You could include some technical points in a review. If it's a film, then think about the acting, directing, script etc.*

*Get your opinions across clearly and support them with examples.*

*The ending should leave the reader in no doubt of your opinion on what you're reviewing.*

# Writing to Inform and Advise

Some questions will ask you to write a text that informs or advises the reader. It sounds a bit tricky, but you'll pick it up as you read these pages. Just make sure you know the differences between them.

## Informing and advising are different things

1) Writing to <u>inform</u> means you need to give someone the <u>facts</u> about something. Tell your reader <u>everything</u> they need to <u>know</u> about the topic you're writing about.

*For some tasks, such as the one below, you'll need to make up these facts. Try to make them sensible and convincing.*

2) Writing to <u>advise</u> means you are trying to help someone with <u>your suggestions</u>. Your writing needs to be <u>clear</u> so that the reader knows <u>what</u> they should do and <u>why</u>.

## Informative writing needs to be full of facts

*This article is for a school magazine, so it could be read by students, teachers and parents. The language should be formal, but it needs to be interesting so that people will read it.*

Write an article for the school magazine to inform readers about a charity event that was organised by your school.

*You're writing to inform, so provide all the important facts. You can make your writing more interesting by giving your opinions.*

On Wednesday 17th April the school organised a sponsored car wash to raise money for the local homeless shelter. Students from Year 10 volunteered to give up their lunch breaks...

*You've got to assume your reader doesn't know what you're writing about. The examiner wants to see how well you can tell them about it.*

*Provide a lot of detail — it will make your writing more informative.*

... The students washed and polished nearly 50 cars, which belonged to teachers and parents. In doing so they raised over £250...

... The homeless shelter that the money was raised for performs a really important service in our community. It does a great job looking after dozens of unfortunate people. The money raised by the school will be used to buy clothing and food for the...

*Try to make what you're writing about sound interesting by giving some of your views.*

## *What a footballer — he's definitely in-form...*

When you're writing non-fiction, make sure you know what style of writing you're meant to be doing, who you're meant to be writing for, and what the aim of your writing is. Then you'll have all the bases covered.

# Writing to Inform and Advise

Take my advice and have a good read of this page...

## Think about the question

*You're giving a speech to your class, so your tone can be quite friendly.*

*You're writing to advise, so you need to give the reader clear, simple guidance.*

Write a speech for your class to advise them about how to make your favourite food.

You need to be careful when making pancakes, because there's always a risk of injury when you cook over a hot stove.

*You can use the word 'you' to appeal directly to your audience.*

*You can also write about your own experiences to make your advice seem more personal.*

In my experience, you get better pancakes if you flip them rather than turning them with a spatula. If nothing else, it's certainly more fun!

Don't be disheartened if your first few pancakes aren't perfect — learning how to make perfect pancakes takes lots of practice, and you'll definitely get it right in the end.

*You could use a reassuring tone to make the audience feel less intimidated.*

## You need to make it clear and interesting

1)  Try to make your writing <u>interesting</u> for the examiner to read — give lots of <u>details</u> and make sure everything you write is <u>clear</u> to follow.

2)  Use plenty of <u>different words</u> rather than the same ones all the time.

3)  Make sure you've done <u>what the question asked</u> and given your information or advice <u>clearly</u>.

If your writing is <u>interesting</u>, you'll pick up <u>more marks</u>. If you <u>sound bored</u>, then you <u>won't</u>.

A glass of water. Clear, but not very interesting.

## Practice Questions

1)  What is the difference between writing to inform and writing to advise?

2)  What should you assume the examiner knows about the topic you're writing about?

3)  Why is it important to make your answer interesting?

4)  Think about your favourite hobby. Jot down some informative points about why you enjoy that hobby and how you feel when you're doing it.

# Writing to Argue and Persuade

Arguing and persuading — that sums up every conversation I have with my parents. Learn how to argue and persuade effectively — it's your one-way ticket to marksville.

## Use evidence to help you argue and persuade

1) When you're writing to <u>argue</u> you need to write <u>clearly</u> and <u>forcefully</u> to show that your <u>opinion</u> is <u>right</u>. You should also think of <u>examples</u> to show <u>how</u> other opinions are <u>wrong</u>, because that will make your argument <u>stronger</u>.

> Write a speech for your class to argue in favour of banning smartphones in school.

← *Try to work out what the other side's arguments would be and think of reasons why they are wrong. Think of examples to support your reasons.*

2) When you're writing to <u>persuade</u> you're often trying to get your reader to <u>do something</u> or <u>think</u> in the <u>same</u> way that you do. You need to write in a way that <u>appeals</u> to your <u>reader</u>.

> Write a letter to a friend to persuade them to come on holiday with you.

← *You're writing to a friend, so you need to use language that will appeal to them and make them really want to join you on holiday.*

3) When you're arguing or persuading you need to think about <u>who</u> you're writing for and use <u>examples</u> that <u>appeal</u> to your reader. This will make your writing more <u>convincing</u> or more <u>persuasive</u>.

## Learn some tricks to improve your writing

1) Pronouns like '<u>we</u>' and '<u>our</u>' can help make your argument sound more <u>convincing</u>.

> <u>We</u> have all heard that...

> <u>Our</u> future depends on...

> The problem <u>we</u> face is...

> This affects <u>us</u> all...

2) Using <u>rhetorical questions</u> is a clever trick that <u>writers</u> and <u>politicians</u> use. You're leaving it to the <u>reader</u> to give the answer, <u>instead</u> of saying it yourself — it's a good way of making them <u>agree with you</u>.

> Is this sort of thing acceptable in our society?

> Why should we put up with this sort of behaviour?

*These are also good things to look out for if you're writing about the language of a non-fiction text (see p.29-30).*

3) A <u>simple</u> and <u>effective</u> way to <u>emphasise</u> your points is to use <u>three describing words</u> in a sentence instead of just <u>one</u>.

> Britain's motorways are <u>expensive</u>, <u>overcrowded</u> and <u>dangerous</u>.

← *This sounds much better than "Britain's motorways are expensive and overcrowded."*

---

## *Paddling in wallets — that's purse-wading...*

Some lovely little tricks to learn here. You can have a go at using 'we' and 'us' to make your answer more personal — and don't forget to use questions and a list of three describing words to emphasise your points.

---

Section Three — Writing Non-Fiction

# Writing to Argue and Persuade

Arguing is all about making people agree with your opinion. So you've got to be really convincing.

## Arguing means showing that you are right

Write an article for your school newspaper to argue in favour of getting rid of school uniforms.

*You've got to argue convincingly to have school uniforms abolished.*

1) When you're trying to <u>argue</u> you need to prove that your opinion is right.

2) You can do this by thinking about the <u>reasons</u> why your opinion is <u>right</u>.

| Reasons why uniforms are bad | Reasons why not having uniforms is good |
|---|---|
| • expensive to buy | • more choice in what to wear |
| • really uncomfortable | • won't get picked on outside of school |
| • not very stylish | • easier to clean non-uniform clothes |

3) Then you can work out ways to <u>attack</u> the <u>opposing arguments</u>. Here are two examples:

> uniforms give a sense of identity — but that's not good if you're identified by a terrible uniform.
>
> uniforms are smart — but not when people don't wear them with pride.

## Use exaggeration to criticise the opposite opinion

1) <u>Exaggerating</u> makes something out to be <u>more</u> than it <u>really is</u>. It's a good way of <u>attacking</u> the <u>opposite opinion</u> to your own.

> The idea that the uniforms give us a sense of identity is a complete fantasy.

2) You <u>don't really mean</u> the idea is a fantasy — it's an over-the-top <u>image</u>.

3) Make sure you give clear, proper <u>reasons</u> to <u>back up</u> your opinion as well. It will make your opinions sound more <u>thoughtful</u> and your argument will be <u>stronger</u>.

*Ah, the old school uniform. We all looked so handsome back then.*

> In fact, the uniform is expensive, uncomfortable and embarrassing to wear, as most students will tell you.

> <u>Don't</u> be <u>rude</u>. Just because you're exaggerating it <u>doesn't mean</u> you can start writing abuse. You <u>won't</u> get good marks if you're mean about people.

## Practice Questions

1) How do pronouns like 'we' and 'our' help to improve your persuasive writing?

2) How can using rhetorical questions in your writing help people to agree with your opinions?

3) Explain how exaggeration can help your argument.

4) Look at a magazine or newspaper article and write down three examples of exaggeration.

# Writing to Argue and Persuade

When you're writing to argue or persuade, you need to get your audience on your side.

## Keep your writing polite

1) It's <u>important</u> to be polite when you're writing about people with the <u>opposite opinion</u> to yours.

> Many people say school uniforms are a necessary part of the education system. However, this opinion ignores the fact that there are very good schools that do not have uniforms.

2) You should just criticise their <u>opinions</u>. <u>Don't</u> criticise them <u>personally</u> — the examiner won't like people who are rude.

## Keep any negative points impersonal

1) If you're going to <u>criticise</u> an <u>opinion</u>, do it <u>without</u> writing about the <u>people</u> who think it.

> A lot of people think school uniforms make everyone equal. They are wrong... ✗

2) This example seems like a <u>personal attack</u> and it makes you sound <u>angry</u>. You <u>won't</u> help your argument by sounding angry.

3) It's <u>much better</u> if you're criticising the <u>opinion</u>, not the <u>people</u>.

> It is often said that school uniforms make everyone equal. This isn't true... ✓

Lara's criticism was always personal.

## Make your positive points personal

1) Make the reader <u>feel</u> that you're all on the <u>same side</u>.

   *Using 'we' makes it sound as if your reader agrees with you already.* → <u>We</u> all believe that individuality is important.

2) You can also use "<u>you</u>" to talk <u>directly</u> to your readers and make your argument more <u>convincing</u>.

> <u>You</u> have a chance to prove that today by getting rid of uniforms.

3) This <u>personal</u> approach might make someone more willing to <u>agree</u> with your argument.

## *It's often said that revision is dull — this isn't true...*

Phew — this positive and negative lark sounds pretty tricky. All it means is you need to stay polite when you make any bad points about the opposite view to yours, and don't attack people — it won't get you marks.

# Writing to Argue and Persuade

Persuading is about trying to get someone to believe that what you're saying is amazing. You've got to really sell something to the reader so that they won't have any doubts about it.

## You've got to make people believe you're right

*Your answer needs to be in the form of a letter and the style needs to be formal, because you're applying for a job.*

You have decided you want to do some volunteer work in your spare time.

Write a letter to the RSPCA persuading them to accept you as a volunteer.

*You need to put your answer in the right style, and make the RSPCA believe that you're right for the job.*

1) When you're trying to <u>persuade</u> someone you should imagine that you're trying to <u>change their minds</u>.

2) A good way to <u>persuade</u> people is to think of all the arguments <u>against</u> your opinion.

> Reasons RSPCA wouldn't accept me:
> - too young — lack of experience
> - not enough free time
> - what could I actually do to help?

3) Then you can work out <u>how</u> to <u>prove</u> those arguments <u>wrong</u>.

> - too young — but <u>parents say it's OK</u>
> - lack of experience — but <u>eager to learn</u> and <u>love animals</u>
> - no time — can <u>arrange to do it</u> at weekends and after school
> - what could I do? — <u>willing to do anything to help</u>.

## You need to be positive

If you sound <u>positive</u> and <u>certain</u> that you're <u>right</u>, people are much <u>more likely</u> to <u>believe</u> you.

Perhaps I might do OK once I've done it for a while.   ✗   *This isn't very positive and it's not very persuasive.*

*This is great because it's really positive and makes you sound confident.*   I am exactly the sort of person you're looking for.   ✓

## Practice Questions

1) Why should you keep your negative points impersonal?

2) How can you make the reader feel that you're all on the same side?

3) Think about something you really want. Jot down three arguments against you having it, and then a reason to prove each argument wrong.

# Planning Your Non-Fiction Writing

This example will help you learn how to tackle the kind of questions you'll face in the exam.

## Work out what the question means

*You're writing for students at your school, so you can write in a fairly conversational style.*

> You have decided that too few students at your school participate in after-school activities.
>
> Write an article for your school newspaper to persuade students at your school to sign up for an after-school activity of your choice.

*You can write about any activity — think of lots of reasons to persuade pupils to join in.*

1) The writing needs to be in the <u>style</u> of a newspaper article, so it should have a <u>headline</u> that <u>summarises</u> the article and captures the reader's <u>attention</u>. You should <u>provide information</u> about the activity. You could include some <u>facts</u> and <u>figures</u> to make your point of view seem <u>reliable</u>.

2) The article is <u>aimed</u> at <u>children</u>, so the <u>language</u> needs to be <u>friendly</u> and <u>exciting</u>. You could use <u>questions</u> or <u>exaggeration</u> to persuade people to join.

3) The aim of the article is to <u>persuade</u>, so it needs to give <u>reasons</u> why people should join the activity.

## Come up with some persuasive ideas in your plan

You can <u>quickly</u> note down <u>reasons</u> to join the activity in a <u>spider diagram</u>.

*For more on planning see p.12-13.*

*You could finish your plan by numbering your reasons, to show which order you're going to put them in your answer.*

Think of some <u>important details</u> that you could include in your article, e.g.

- When the activity is held.
- How long the activity takes.
- What the activity costs.

You can <u>make up</u> these details, but they should be <u>sensible</u>.

# Worked Answer

This example answer will give you some ideas on how to write a non-fiction text.

## Start off with a cracking introduction

Your <u>introduction</u> needs to get the attention of the reader.

*Using rhetorical questions is a good way of making the reader agree with you.*

Athletics — a fun way to keep fit and make friends

Do you feel as if you're not getting enough exercise? Do you want to make new friends? Are you looking for something that's free and fun to do? If your answer is 'yes' to any of these, then it's your lucky day.

*You should write a heading for your article. The wording should draw attention to your text — this one emphasises the key points of the article.*

## You need to persuade the reader

Make your writing as <u>persuasive</u> as possible.

*Mentioning things like 'health problems' might persuade people to join up because they want to stay healthy.*

At the end of school, we all want to go home and relax. But sitting in front of the television for hours doesn't do any of us any good. Doctors recommend that teenagers spend two hours a week exercising. If you don't, then you can develop health problems. Sign up for athletics because, in return for a small amount of your time, you can get the exercise you need.

*Giving facts like this makes your argument more convincing.*

*Directly addressing the reader makes the argument more persuasive.*

Here's another example:

*This kind of language reassures the reader and makes them feel more comfortable.*

Don't worry if you feel that you're not the best at sport. The club is set up for people of all abilities so that anyone can join. There are plenty of different sports you could try, such as running, shot put or long jump. Just see which one suits you best. It's all about having fun and trying new things, so there's no need to feel uncomfortable.

*Positive language makes the activity more appealing.*

## Finish off with a strong conclusion

<u>Summarise</u> the <u>main points</u> of the article and <u>encourage</u> them to join.

*You could summarise the main ideas in your final paragraph.*

So why not sign up for after-school athletics? It's only two hours of your time each Wednesday, it'll help you to keep fit and, best of all, you'll have a lot of fun. Join after-school athletics today, for absolutely no charge at all. It might just change your life.

*End with something positive.*

# Planning Your Creative Writing

You've got to plan your creative writing.  I know, I'm beginning to sound like a broken record...  What's a record?  You know — round black shiny discs, came before cassettes.  What are cassettes?  Good grief.

## There are lots of different types of creative writing

For some <u>creative writing</u> questions, you might be asked to write a <u>story</u>, <u>part</u> of a story (i.e. the opening or ending) or a <u>description</u> of something.  Here are some <u>example questions</u>.

> Write about a time when you were afraid.

> Write the opening part of a story about somewhere dangerous.

> Write a story with the title 'The Wave'.

> Write a description suggested by the picture below... ◀┈┈

*Some questions won't specify a particular type of writing.  For these, you should aim to be descriptive <u>and</u> tell a story.*

*For some questions, you'll be given one or more pictures to inspire your writing.*

## Planning creative writing is just like planning an essay

1) If you get to <u>choose</u> your creative writing question, <u>think</u> about your options before diving in.

2) It's really <u>important</u> to <u>plan</u> creative writing, but remember to keep your plan quite <u>short</u>, make sure it's <u>relevant</u> to the question, and try to <u>bring it to life</u> when you start writing.

## First you need to think of something to write about

1) Think of <u>ideas</u> that <u>fit the question</u>, and <u>scribble</u> them down.

> Write about a time when you were afraid.

- Lost in supermarket — possible but boring
- Stuck on mountain when friend broke his leg climbing — add some extra details

*Norris felt afraid as he tiptoed through, but he was pretty sure Frank would get eaten first.*

2) You've got to <u>work out</u> exactly what <u>happens</u> in the story <u>before</u> you start writing.  Write down <u>who's</u> in it, <u>what</u> happens and <u>what feelings</u> you're going to describe.

- About being <u>afraid</u>: me, Steve, Pete & Joe
- Trapped on mountain;  bad weather;  no one else about;  had some food, but not enough warm clothes — cold & hungry — worried
- Steve in pain — first aid (others went for help)

## *This page is absolutely plantastic...*

Your plan will help make sure that you don't get distracted or forget anything.  I once forgot my shoes because I was distracted — I got some really funny looks walking to the shops.  What was I saying again...

# Starting Your Story

Badgers can dig holes twice as fast as a human can run...  Just kidding, but it did grab your attention.  Make the beginning of your story really gripping and memorable and you'll get more marks.

## Grab your reader's attention

It's always a good idea to <u>start</u> your stories with a <u>sentence</u> that'll make your reader want to <u>carry on reading</u>.  For example:

1) You could start with a <u>direct address</u> to the reader:

> You've never seen a ghost before, have you?

*This grabs the reader's attention by speaking to them directly.*

2) Or you could introduce an <u>unusual</u> or <u>interesting character</u>:

> Josephina Fawkes had only two interests in life — knitting and fighting crime.

*This makes the reader want to know more about the character.*

## Start your stories in the middle of the action

1) Your writing needs to keep the reader <u>interested</u> and make the story <u>come to life</u>.

2) <u>Start</u> your story in the <u>middle</u> of the <u>action</u> to really <u>grip</u> your reader.

> Write a story about a time when you wish you had acted differently.

> Once, many years ago, when I was a lot younger, we were on holiday in Spain.  There were all sorts of exciting things there, and we were having a really good time.

*This is seriously dull.  It doesn't jump out at you or grab your attention.*

> I couldn't believe it.  He was gone. "He must be here somewhere," I thought to myself, as I went through the shed, desperately picking up boxes and throwing them aside.  It was no use.  Peter had run away and it was all my fault.

*This is much better.  It starts in the middle of the action and makes you want to read on.*

3) The <u>last sentence</u> makes it <u>clear</u> that the story <u>is</u> about 'a time when you wish you had acted differently'.  It shows that the story is definitely <u>answering</u> the question.

### Practice Questions

1) Name three things that you have to decide when you're planning a story.

2) Write a short plan to answer this question:
'Write about a time when you were proud of yourself.'

3) Write the first paragraph of an answer to this question:
'Write a story about being a teenager.'

# Improving Your Story

My teacher once told me that writing a story is a bit like a race. You've got to start well, keep going in the middle, and then finish well. This page is about writing well in the middle of the race. I'm getting mixed up.

## Make your words fit the task

Try to <u>change</u> the <u>language</u> you use to fit the <u>style</u> of writing you're going for.

1) If you were writing a <u>spooky</u> story, you'd use descriptive, <u>scary</u> language like this:

> *The door screeched open and I carefully entered the dingy cellar. Shadows cast by my torch leapt up at me through the gloom.* ←

*The words 'screeched', 'dingy' and 'gloom' make this writing sound spooky.*

2) If it's an <u>adventure</u> story, you'd use <u>exciting</u> and <u>dramatic</u> language like this:

> *I burst noisily through the thicket of trees and sprinted towards the shore. The men were still chasing me, bellowing threats.* ←

*There's plenty of action in this writing. Words like 'burst' and 'sprinted' make it sound exciting.*

## Practise writing in the first person and in the third person

1) If you write a story as if <u>you're</u> the <u>main character</u>, you're using the <u>first person</u> (your story has a <u>first-person narrative</u>). It helps the reader <u>imagine</u> that the story is happening to <u>them</u>.

> *I wandered slowly to the park. I was so bored.* ←

*The narrator is one of the characters in the story — it's written in the first person.*

2) If you write a story about a <u>group of characters</u>, but you're <u>not involved</u>, you're writing in the <u>third person</u> (your story has a <u>third-person narrative</u>). You can write about the thoughts and feelings of <u>all</u> the characters by writing in the <u>third person</u>.

> *Juliet wandered slowly to the park. She was so bored.* ←

*The narrator isn't one of the characters — it's written in the third person.*

## Keep your writing focused

1) <u>Don't</u> try to include <u>too much</u> in your writing. You probably only need to write about one or two <u>main events</u>.

2) Make sure everything you write is <u>relevant</u> to the <u>question</u>. It's good to include <u>detail</u>, but make sure you don't <u>waffle</u>.

3) This is where it'll help to have a <u>good plan</u> — and <u>stick</u> to it. Then you won't get <u>side-tracked</u>.

*Marty's new glasses allowed him to focus on his fashion line 'Bags for Life'.*

---

### *First-person perspective — what the front of the queue looks like...*

Try to bring your creative writing to life with descriptive language and interesting images. Don't just say 'This happened... then this happened... then this happened'. Describe feelings, places and situations instead.

# Ending Your Story

There's nothing worse than a story with no ending. I once took a book on holiday that completely gripped me. I was reading it by the pool one day when a gigantic crocodile suddenly leapt up out of the water and

## Your story needs a powerful ending

To leave a really good impression on the examiner, your story needs to have an <u>interesting ending</u>. Here are some <u>ideas</u>:

- You could show the <u>main character</u> coming to some kind of <u>realisation</u>.

- You could create a <u>cliffhanger</u> ending by finishing with a <u>question</u>. This will leave the reader thinking about what will happen <u>next</u>.

- You could have a <u>neat</u>, <u>happy ending</u> that will <u>satisfy</u> the reader.

## You could end a story with a surprise

A really <u>dramatic way</u> to end a story is with an <u>unexpected twist</u>.

*Don't write "Then I woke up — it was all a dream!" It's dull, dull, dull.*

> I knew I should never have stolen the vase, so I took it to the cliff and threw it over, watching it smash on the rocks below. I thought my guilty secret was gone forever.
>
> Late that night, the wind was howling around my tent, and the rain was pouring down. There was a huge crash of thunder and a bright flash of lightning. Terrified, I ran out of the tent. There, sitting on top of a tree stump, was the missing vase. It was completely whole. I looked around and saw the old man walking slowly away.

This is a very <u>exciting</u> ending, because everything is left <u>unexplained</u>.

## Leave yourself enough time for the ending

Leave <u>plenty of time</u> to write your <u>ending</u>. If you find you're <u>running out</u> of time, <u>think up</u> a <u>quick</u> ending.

> It was too late. I realised I had spent it all.
>
> I tried to keep it a secret but my parents found out eventually, and I ended up in lots of trouble. Even now I still feel guilty. My parents still don't trust me with money. I wish I hadn't taken that cash.

*Just put what happened in the end.*

*Then write about how it makes you feel now. Make sure it's relevant to the question.*

### Practice Questions

1) What kind of language would you use in an adventure story?

2) What does 'writing in the third person' mean?

3) Find a paragraph in a novel or short story that's written in the third person. Rewrite the paragraph in the first person.

4) Write a plan for an adventure story with the title 'The Mysterious Island' and then write out its dramatic last paragraph.

# Writing Descriptions

Some questions ask you to describe — that means saying what something is like or how something feels.

## Keep your descriptions interesting

Lots of questions ask you to <u>describe</u> things. Like this one:

> You are going to submit a piece of writing
> to a creative writing anthology about travel.
> Write a description of a journey.

*The way to do well in questions like these is to make your description as interesting to read as possible.*

This one:

> Describe an occasion where you felt angry or upset.
> Focus on your thoughts and feelings.

*This question specifically asks for a description of your thoughts and feelings. You could use imagery to describe the feelings (see next page).*

Or this one:

> Write a description suggested
> by the picture of a forest below.

*For this question you need to write a description inspired by a specific image. It'd be a good idea to write in the third person (see p.52).*

## Be careful how you use words

<u>Don't</u> use the <u>same words</u>, like 'interesting' and 'beautiful', all the time — it's really <u>dull</u>.

> It was a <u>fascinating</u> train trip,
> through miles of <u>fascinating</u> desert.
> I met lots of <u>fascinating</u> people too...

*Especially avoid using the word "nice" too much — it can make your writing sound really bland.*

This clown kept using the same describing words.

You need to find <u>different words</u> to <u>describe</u> everything — you're trying to help the reader <u>imagine</u> what the journey was <u>like</u>.

> It was a <u>fascinating</u> train trip, through miles of
> <u>empty</u> desert. I met lots of <u>entertaining</u> people too...

*This is much better. It's a lot more interesting to read.*

Try to add some <u>extra information</u> to <u>back up</u> what you're saying. It makes your writing more <u>entertaining</u>, <u>engaging</u> and <u>varied</u> — which are all things that the <u>examiner</u> will give <u>marks</u> for.

> Climbing a mountain can be torturous, <u>because</u> the thin air makes it hard to breathe.

*If you back up your describing words then you'll make your description clearer to understand.*

> The sense of relief when you reach the summit is overwhelming
> <u>because</u> you have worked so hard to get there.

## *What a wondrous, marvellous, splendiferous page this is...*

If you're describing a place or a scene, think about all five of the senses. Describing what things smell, taste, feel or sound like, as well as what they look like, will bring your writing to life and impress the examiner.

# Writing Descriptions

There are a few other things you can do to improve your marks for describing questions, but I'm not going to tell you about them. Oh wait... what's that? We've got a whole page on them? Foiled again...

## Use images to bring your writing to life

1) Images are <u>word pictures</u> — they make your writing <u>more descriptive</u>.

> The coach lurched forward <u>like</u> a dog chasing a stick.

*When you describe something as being like something else it's called a simile.*

2) You can also <u>compare</u> things using "<u>as</u>" — "as beautiful as", "as gentle as" etc.

> The rooster on her lap was <u>as</u> big <u>as</u> a Christmas turkey.

*This is also a simile.*

3) You can write that something actually <u>is</u> something else.

> Her eyes were blue, glittering sapphires.

*This is a metaphor.*

Her eyes <u>aren't</u> really sapphires, they're <u>like</u> sapphires. This is just a <u>dramatic</u> way of saying it.

## Avoid using clichés

Clichés are <u>phrases</u> or <u>images</u> that have been <u>used so often</u> they've become <u>boring</u>.

> He is as hard as nails.

> Football is a game of two halves.

> He's as good as gold.

> You win some, you lose some.

> It was as dead as a dodo.

> I'll sweeten the deal.

Try <u>not</u> to use them in your descriptions — you don't want to make your writing <u>dull</u>.

## Don't use slang or jargon words

1) <u>Slang</u> is the sort of language you use with your mates. You shouldn't use it in your descriptions — the examiner <u>might not know</u> what you <u>mean</u>.

2) <u>Jargon</u> is any sort of <u>technical term</u> that most people <u>wouldn't</u> understand, like <u>sports terms</u> or <u>police terms</u> from TV. Only use them if you <u>explain</u> what they <u>mean</u>.

"Verily, I adore spending time with my chums. We always have a spiffing time together."

> He's crashing and I need a ventilator, stat!  = medical jargon.

> Hostiles are flanking us to the west of the LZ.  = military jargon.

## Practice Questions

1) Why shouldn't you use the same words all the time in your descriptive writing?

2) How does extra information improve your descriptions?

3) Describe your weekend in three paragraphs. Use different words to describe what you did, and include at least one image in your writing.

**Section Four — Creative Writing**

# Writing Descriptions

Describing questions often don't give you a clear question to answer. The trick is to grab the examiner's attention and give them a really clear mental picture of the thing or experience you're describing.

## Some questions will give you images to write about

You might have to write a description that's inspired by a picture. Here's an example question.

You have decided to enter a creative writing competition.
Your entry will be judged by a panel of professional writers.
Write a description suggested by this picture:

*Some exam boards will give you more than one picture to base your answer on — make sure you read the question carefully before you start writing.*

*Use interesting adjectives in your descriptions.*

*Impress the examiner by using unusual imagery to describe the scene.*

Blazing lights illuminated the actor as she stood elegantly on the empty stage. The clear sound of her voice rang across the theatre, sweeping over the audience of jewel-red seats before her, each one sat in stunned silence at the sound of her stirring soliloquy.

## Sometimes you'll have to imagine what you're describing

If you answer a question that doesn't come with a picture, you'll need to use your imagination to come up with some things to write about.

Think of a town or city that you know well.
Describe what you like best about it.

*You need to pick somewhere you're really familiar with and make sure that you have plenty to write about.*

The best thing about New York is how beautiful it looks after dark. In the evening you can stand in the park and look at the glittering lights on the buildings, which shine like stars. It can be busy and stressful during the daytime, but at night it's as peaceful as a sleeping animal, resting quietly before it comes to life again in the morning.

*Descriptive language should give the reader a clear idea of what you're talking about.*

*Use similes to give the reader a sense of the atmosphere in the place you're describing.*

## *Be extra creative — use a different colour for each letter...*

Practise creative writing by lining up all your pens on your desk in colour order, then start writing. I'm just kidding — this won't help at all. I'm not kidding about the practice though — that'll definitely help you.

# An Example of Creative Writing

This page shows an answer all the way from the planning stage to the ending. But as my grandmother used to say — 'you'll never write anything unless you write something'... Or was it 'practice makes perfect'...

## Here's an example of a creative writing question

You <u>might</u> have to answer a question <u>like this</u>.

> You've been asked to write a piece for a creative writing website. Write a short story that has the theme 'Choices'.

Read through the <u>plan</u> below.

- Can win a prize by buying biscuits in the supermarket
- Only two packets left (rich tea and custard creams) so has to choose
- Doesn't win anything — someone who chooses other biscuits wins £1 million
- The winner's life is ruined — they don't know who their real friends are
- Narrator has luck in other ways

## Here's the first paragraph of the answer

Once you've made your <u>plan</u>, it's time to <u>start writing</u>.

> Losing a million pounds was the best thing that ever happened to me. I didn't realise it at the time, of course. The day I made the choice that changed my life, I trudged away from the supermarket feeling like the unluckiest girl in the world. In reality, though, I'd had a very narrow escape.

*This first sentence is gripping because it's unexpected — normally losing money would make people unhappy. This makes the reader want to read on to find out why it doesn't in this case.*

## Here's the last paragraph of the answer

1) The story should <u>explain</u> what <u>happened</u> and how the <u>choice</u> affected the main character's <u>life</u>.

2) The <u>last</u> paragraph should <u>refer back</u> to the <u>question</u> or <u>theme</u>.

> If I'd chosen the other packet of biscuits and won the money, I would never have met my best friend, never have saved that dog from the fire and never have spent a year travelling the world. It's funny how such a small choice can affect your life in such a big way. Now I always choose custard creams — just in case.

*This final paragraph links back to the theme of 'choices'.*

*The last sentence leaves the reader with the idea that something like this could happen again.*

### Practice Questions

1) "You should ignore small details when describing a picture" — true or false?

2) Write down your own plan for a different short story with the theme 'Choices'.

3) Describe the five most interesting things about one of your friends.

# Ten Writing Tips

Phew — there's a lot of advice stuffed into this book. I didn't think that was enough, though, so I've filled this page with cracking tips that'll improve your writing. There's a joke too, but I'd ignore that if I were you.

① **Read the instructions** → Read the front of the paper so you know what you have to do — how many questions you'll have to answer and how much time you have.

② **Read the question** →
- Read the question thoroughly. Make sure you understand it.
- If there are a few different parts to the question, make sure you answer all of them.

③ **Plan your answer** → If it's an essay or a long writing task, do some planning. Jot down any ideas you have. Put them in an order that makes sense.

④ **New point — new paragraph** → Put each new point in a new paragraph. Use linking words and phrases to link your paragraphs together.

⑤ **Use P.E.E.D. in your answers** →
- Make a Point.
- Back it up with an Example, e.g. a quote.
- Explain how the example backs up your point.
- Develop your point.

⑥ **When you're answering writing questions, remember — What? Who? Why?** →
- What type of writing is it — e.g. a letter.
- Who are you writing for — e.g. the council.
- Why are you writing — e.g. to persuade.

⑦ **Answer the question** → Make sure you answer the question. Keep looking back at the question to make sure you've stayed on track.

⑧ **Compare texts** → If you're asked to compare two texts, discuss their similarities and differences.

⑨ **Don't contradict yourself** → Try not to say one thing is true and then say the opposite is true. It sounds confusing.

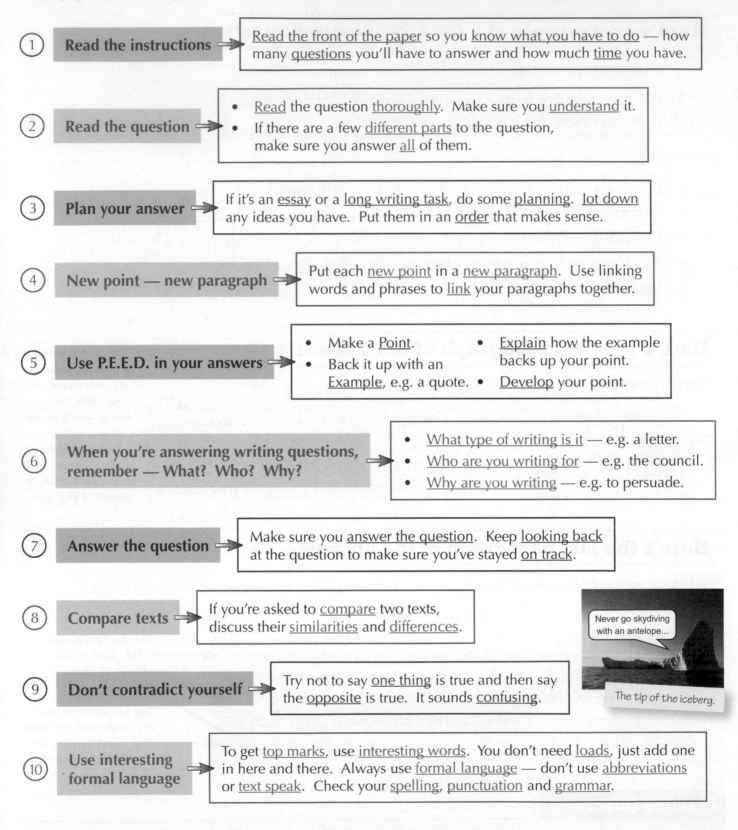

Never go skydiving with an antelope...

The tip of the iceberg.

⑩ **Use interesting formal language** → To get top marks, use interesting words. You don't need loads, just add one in here and there. Always use formal language — don't use abbreviations or text speak. Check your spelling, punctuation and grammar.

---

## And now, the end is here — and so I face, the final page-turn...

If you know these ten tips, you'll be well on your way to scoring some cracking marks in your English GCSEs. So that's my last piece of advice to you — learn them off by heart. That's it from me, then. Toodle pip.

# Index

## A

advising (writing) 42, 43
arguing (essays) 20, 21
arguing (writing) 44-47
articles (writing) 40, 42, 45, 48, 49
articles (writing about) 26, 29, 30
audience 13, 31, 40, 41, 43, 46

## B

background information 6
balanced argument 21
bullet points 27, 32, 34

## C

characters 11, 31, 33, 51
choosing questions 10
clichés 55
cliffhangers 53
comparing 9, 11, 16, 24-26, 30, 34, 36, 37, 58
conclusions 2, 3, 14, 22, 23, 39, 49
content 15
contradicting yourself 21, 58
conversational style 40, 48
creative writing 50-57

## D

descriptions 50, 54-56
descriptive language 15, 27, 28, 41, 52, 56
direct address 51
dramatic language 52, 53

## E

effect (of language) 4, 5, 11, 26, 27, 30, 31, 34, 35
embedded quotes 6, 7, 28
ending stories 53
essays 3, 5, 14, 18-23, 32, 33, 38, 39
evaluating 2, 26, 28
exaggeration 13, 45, 48
examples 3-7, 12, 14, 30, 32-35, 37, 38, 44
exams 1-3, 10, 12, 31, 48
explaining words and phrases 8
extra information 54

## F

facts 26, 42, 48, 49
first person 52
five senses 54
form 40
formal language 8, 40-42, 58

## G

generalising 21
grab attention 18, 40, 51

## H

headlines 40, 41, 48, 49
hidden meaning 15
however and therefore 9

## I

imagery 15, 36-39, 55, 56
informal language 15
informing (writing) 42, 43
instructions 58
introductions 2, 3, 13, 14, 18, 19, 39, 49

## J

jargon 55

## L

language 2, 5, 11, 13, 15, 26, 27, 30, 34, 38, 39, 48, 49, 52, 55
leaflets 5, 11, 41
letters 11, 40, 44, 47
linking 9, 16, 17, 24, 33, 37, 58
lists 16, 26

## M

main events 52
main idea 3, 14-16, 19, 20, 35, 36, 38, 39
metaphors 55
mood 15, 26, 35

# Index

EER42